THE

POWER

OF

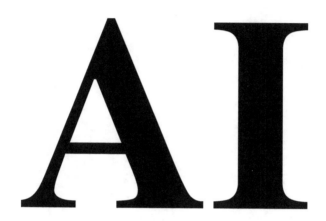

AI

FIRST EDITION

An Easy Beginner's Guide to Understanding and Using Artificial Intelligence

No Formulas, No Tech Overload — Just Practical Tools to Improve Your Life

MASTERPLANNERS
2025

Table of Contents

SECTION 1: WHAT IS AI AND WHY IT MATTERS

SECTION 2: AI IN YOUR DAILY LIFE

● SECTION 3: AI AT WORK AND IN BUSINESS

● SECTION 4: CREATIVE AND PERSONAL EXPRESSION THROUGH AI

● SECTION 5: RISKS, ETHICS & THE FUTURE OF AI

SECTION 1

WHAT IS AI AND WHY IT MATTERS

(Understanding the basics without the tech overwhelm)

What Is Artificial Intelligence?

When most people hear the words "Artificial Intelligence," they might picture robots from movies or complicated computer programs full of mysterious numbers and symbols. But AI is actually much simpler and more practical than most imagine. Put plainly, artificial intelligence is when computers or machines mimic human thinking to solve problems, make decisions, or complete tasks. It's a bit like teaching your smartphone or computer to think—or at least act—like a person.

At its core, AI is about helping technology learn patterns from data. Imagine you have a basket of different fruits. After showing you enough apples, oranges, and bananas, you'll quickly learn to recognize each fruit instantly. AI works the same way. It looks at lots of examples—such as pictures, sounds, or numbers—learns what those examples mean, and then applies this learning to recognize similar situations. This process is known as "machine learning," and it's how apps like Netflix recommend shows you might like, or your phone recognizes your face to unlock the screen.

How AI Actually Works

AI doesn't really "think" the way people do—it doesn't have feelings, intuition, or imagination. Instead, it follows clear instructions called algorithms, step-by-step rules computers use to solve problems. To get a feel for this, consider how you'd bake a cake. You'd follow a recipe, measure ingredients carefully, and bake at the right temperature. AI does something similar but with information instead of flour and eggs. It gathers data, looks for patterns, learns from those patterns, and then makes decisions based on what it's learned.

Here's a simple example:

You: "Hey Siri, what's the weather like tomorrow?"
AI's Steps:

1. Recognize your voice and translate it into text.

2. Understand the meaning of your request.

3. Retrieve weather data from the internet.

4. Convert this data into understandable speech.

5. Respond clearly, saying something like, "It will be sunny and 75 degrees."

This entire process takes seconds, but behind it are carefully coded instructions that tell Siri exactly how to act at each step.

📌 Common Types of AI in Daily Life

To make AI even simpler, let's break it down into some common everyday examples:

AI Technology	Simple Explanation
Voice Assistants (Siri, Alexa)	They understand speech and perform tasks you ask for, such as setting alarms, making calls, or answering questions.
Social Media Algorithms	AI learns your preferences and suggests content (videos, posts) you might enjoy based on your activity.
Navigation Apps (Google Maps)	AI finds the fastest route and helps you avoid traffic by analyzing live road conditions.
Email Filters (Gmail, Outlook)	AI automatically separates spam or promotional emails from important messages by analyzing content patterns.

Notice that AI doesn't always mean "robots." It can be something as simple and helpful as suggesting a song you might like or alerting you that it's time to leave home because traffic is building up.

How Smart Is AI Really?

AI can be extremely good at certain tasks, especially those involving clear rules, large amounts of data, and repetitive activities. However, there are things AI still can't do well. It doesn't truly "understand" context or emotions in the way people do. For example, while AI can help you find songs that match your past music choices, it can't know how you're feeling today unless you specifically tell it.

Here's a quick look at what AI can and cannot handle effectively today:

- **AI can:**
  - Recognize faces and objects in images
  - Predict shopping trends based on data
  - Translate languages quickly and efficiently
  - Drive cars under controlled conditions

- **AI struggles to:**
  - Fully understand human emotions or sarcasm
  - Create completely original, creative ideas without guidance
  - Adapt instantly to unexpected situations without data
  - Handle tasks that require deep empathy or complex moral judgments

This doesn't make AI less valuable—just realistic. AI complements human skills but doesn't replace them entirely.

▶ Common Misunderstandings About AI

There are a few common myths about AI worth clearing up right away:

- **Myth:** AI will soon replace all human jobs. **Reality:** AI automates repetitive tasks but also creates new jobs and requires human oversight.

- **Myth:** AI always knows the right answer. **Reality:** AI makes mistakes, especially if given incorrect or biased information.

- **Myth:** AI systems are always neutral and fair. **Reality:** AI can reflect biases from data it learns from, which may unintentionally discriminate or make unfair choices.

Understanding AI realistically means appreciating both its benefits and its limitations.

📖 Summing It All Up Clearly

Artificial Intelligence is a powerful tool that makes technology smarter and more helpful in our daily lives. It's designed to mimic human thinking—learning from examples, recognizing patterns, and making decisions—but it doesn't actually think or feel emotions. AI enhances how we shop, communicate, navigate, and learn, and it will only continue to grow more useful over time.

Remember, AI is simply another form of intelligence, one created by people, for people. Instead of fearing it or overestimating it, seeing AI clearly as a helpful companion rather than an intimidating force makes it easier to embrace.

📖 A Brief History of AI: From Sci-Fi to Smartphone

Artificial Intelligence might seem like a brand-new concept, especially since it's making headlines nearly every day now. But AI didn't appear overnight. Its story began long before smartphones or smart speakers were even imagined. To truly appreciate how AI affects your life today, it helps to take a brief trip back through its fascinating journey—from futuristic stories to everyday reality.

The idea of intelligent machines actually dates back thousands of years. Ancient Greek myths told of bronze robots that guarded islands, and medieval legends featured mechanical men. But real-life AI, as we think of it today, started to become a realistic goal only about 70 years ago, after the invention of modern computers. Let's walk step-by-step through how AI evolved from an imaginative idea into practical technology that fits neatly in your pocket.

📌 Early Dreams: AI in Science Fiction (1900s-1950s)

The idea of intelligent machines first took hold in people's imaginations through novels and movies. In the early 20th century, fiction writers and filmmakers dreamed about robots and computers with human-like intelligence. These stories made people wonder if machines could ever think, feel, or even act independently.

In 1927, the movie *Metropolis* showed a robot that looked human and could mimic people's behavior. Later, famous authors like Isaac Asimov and Philip K. Dick explored AI extensively in their stories, creating scenarios where robots interacted closely with humans, raising important questions about ethics and humanity.

These fictional visions were important because they inspired scientists and engineers to explore what was possible. Even today, many of our ideas about AI come from those early stories and films.

💡 **Quick fact:** Isaac Asimov introduced the famous "Three Laws of Robotics" in 1942, which many modern AI developers still reference when considering ethical challenges.

⚙️ The Birth of AI as a Science (1950s-1960s)

AI moved from fiction into real-world science during the 1950s. In 1950, British mathematician Alan Turing famously asked, "Can machines think?" He developed a simple test—now known as the "Turing Test"—to see if a machine could mimic human conversation convincingly enough to fool people into believing it was human.

Then, in 1956, researchers organized the first-ever conference specifically on Artificial Intelligence at Dartmouth College. Scientists believed that creating thinking machines might be fairly straightforward. Early enthusiasm was high, and researchers quickly began developing simple programs capable of tasks like solving basic math problems, playing checkers, and answering simple questions.

Early AI Milestones:

Year	Event	Importance
1950	Alan Turing proposes the "Turing Test"	First real-world test of AI
1956	Dartmouth AI Conference	Official birth of AI research
1959	"Logic Theorist" solves math proofs	AI proves it can solve problems

But reality soon tempered their optimism. Computers of the time were slow, expensive, and had limited memory. AI progress, initially promising, soon stalled due to technical challenges.

⚠ The AI Winter: When Dreams Cooled Off (1970s-1980s)

After early excitement, AI ran into trouble. Expectations were high, but results didn't match them. Computers simply weren't powerful enough yet to handle the complexity researchers dreamed of. Funding dried up, research slowed dramatically, and the period known as the "AI Winter" began.

This "winter" wasn't all bad, though. Researchers learned important lessons. They realized AI required more than just logic—it needed better computing power and more data. During these decades, the focus shifted quietly to foundational technologies, laying the groundwork for future breakthroughs.

🚀 The Revival of AI: New Approaches & Computing Power (1990s-2000s)

AI started to thaw out during the 1990s and 2000s. Computers grew faster, cheaper, and capable of storing massive amounts of information. Suddenly, AI projects once considered impossible became realistic again.

One of the biggest milestones came in 1997, when IBM's Deep Blue computer defeated the world chess champion, Garry Kasparov. This made headlines around the globe and proved AI could outperform humans in highly specialized tasks.

In the early 2000s, breakthroughs in machine learning—the process of teaching computers to learn patterns from data—began transforming AI. The internet boom provided massive datasets that fueled new innovations in recognizing images, understanding speech, and predicting user preferences.

▦ AI Enters Everyday Life (2010-Present)

The modern AI era truly took off around 2010. Companies like Google, Amazon, Apple, and Microsoft heavily invested in AI research, pushing technologies into consumer products that millions use every day.

Think about it: Siri debuted in 2011, offering millions of users their first daily experience with conversational AI. Amazon's Alexa arrived in homes in 2014, quickly followed by smart home gadgets that used AI to automate lighting, heating, and security.

AI didn't stop there. Apps like Uber and Netflix relied heavily on AI to offer personalized experiences. Social media giants like Facebook and Instagram used sophisticated AI algorithms to show users content they'd most likely enjoy.

Everyday Application	AI Behind the Scenes
Netflix Recommendations	AI analyzes viewing patterns and suggests new shows
FaceID on iPhones	AI quickly and accurately recognizes your face
Amazon Shopping	AI predicts products based on your browsing history

Now, AI is even in healthcare, finance, education, and customer service—becoming invisible but essential to modern life.

The Future: What's Next for AI?

Today, AI is still rapidly evolving. Researchers are developing smarter, more versatile AI tools like ChatGPT —machines capable of holding complex conversations, creating artwork, or helping write content (like this book!).

Yet AI also faces new challenges. Questions about ethics, fairness, and privacy are becoming increasingly urgent. Governments, companies, and individuals must navigate how AI affects jobs, personal freedoms, and even democracy itself.

The next step in AI evolution isn't just about more powerful technology. It's about responsible and thoughtful use. AI will undoubtedly continue reshaping the world, but the direction it takes depends largely on us—the creators and users.

AI vs Machine Learning vs Neural Networks

Artificial Intelligence, Machine Learning, and Neural Networks. You've probably heard these terms thrown around together, often interchangeably. It's easy to get confused—aren't they all basically the same thing? Not exactly. While these ideas are closely connected, understanding how they're different helps you use AI tools more effectively and talk about AI with clarity.

To keep things simple:

- **Artificial Intelligence (AI)** is the big picture—the general idea of computers doing tasks that normally require human thinking.

- **Machine Learning (ML)** is a specific approach used within AI, where computers learn from data without explicit instructions for every single step.

- **Neural Networks** are a specialized, powerful type of ML inspired by how the human brain works.

Let's explore each of these clearly, step by step, so you can confidently discuss, use, and even explain AI to others.

📌 Artificial Intelligence (AI): The Big Picture

At the highest level, Artificial Intelligence means computers or machines acting in ways that seem intelligent—doing tasks like solving problems, recognizing objects, or responding to questions. AI covers a wide range of activities, from simple things like your phone recommending songs you might enjoy, to complex tasks like self-driving cars navigating through busy city streets.

AI doesn't refer to any one specific technology. Instead, it's an umbrella term covering many methods, all aiming to create machines that act smartly. Imagine AI as the entire toolbox, filled with different techniques and technologies used to achieve intelligent behaviors.

Examples of everyday AI:

Application	How it Uses AI
Virtual Assistants	Understand your voice and respond intelligently (Siri, Alexa)
Online Recommendations	Suggest products, movies, or music based on your past choices
Self-driving Cars	Navigate roads and obstacles autonomously

Simply put: AI is the concept. Everything else fits within that idea.

◎ Machine Learning (ML): Learning from Experience

Machine Learning is a key method used to create AI systems. If AI is the toolbox, ML is one specific tool inside that toolbox—perhaps the most popular and powerful one today.

ML allows computers to learn from data, discover patterns, and make decisions without explicit instructions telling them exactly what to do each time. Think of ML like training a puppy. At first, your puppy doesn't know any commands. You give treats and praise every time the puppy sits, teaching it that this action earns a reward. Over time, your puppy learns to sit whenever asked—without needing continuous instructions or rewards every single time.

ML works similarly. You provide data (examples), the system analyzes it, finds patterns, and uses these patterns to make future decisions or predictions. For instance, ML powers spam filters, which get better at identifying unwanted emails the more examples they see.

Real-life ML examples:

- **Netflix Recommendations:** ML analyzes millions of viewing choices and patterns to suggest new shows you'll probably enjoy.

- **Email Filtering (Gmail):** ML learns what you consider spam or important, automatically sorting emails effectively.

- **Fraud Detection:** Banks use ML to detect unusual spending patterns and alert you to potential fraud.

ML thrives when there's plenty of data and clear outcomes it can learn from. It's powerful but also limited by the quality of the data it receives. If the data is biased or incomplete, the system's decisions can reflect these problems too.

🧠 Neural Networks: The Human-Brain Inspired Technique

Neural Networks are a special, highly sophisticated type of Machine Learning. They get their name because their structure is loosely inspired by the human brain—specifically, the network of neurons (nerve cells) we use to think, learn, and recognize patterns.

A neural network consists of interconnected "nodes" (similar to neurons) organized into layers. Each node processes data and passes information forward.

These layers analyze the input (such as images or sound), detect patterns, and produce accurate results.

Think of a neural network like a team of experts, each responsible for one small part of a bigger task. For example, if the task is recognizing images, one layer might recognize edges or shapes, another identifies colors or textures, and another layer recognizes complete objects like faces or cars.

Example: How Neural Networks Recognize Faces

Layer	What it does
Layer 1	Detect edges and simple shapes
Layer 2	Identify facial features (eyes, noses, mouths)
Layer 3	Recognize whole faces from the combined features

Neural Networks are behind many impressive AI breakthroughs in recent years, from voice recognition (Siri) and image recognition (Google Photos tagging) to more advanced tasks like real-time translation and medical diagnosis.

However, they need huge amounts of data to train effectively and are often harder to understand because their internal logic can become extremely complex.

 How AI, ML, and Neural Networks Fit Together

It helps to visualize how these three concepts connect:

- **Artificial Intelligence:**
  The big idea: Machines performing tasks we think of as intelligent.

- **Machine Learning:**
  One method within AI: Computers learn from data

and improve performance without explicit instructions.

- **Neural Networks:**
  A specific ML method: Complex systems inspired by the human brain, excelling at tasks like recognition and complex decision-making.

Here's a simple chart to make it clear:

Artificial Intelligence (AI)

└── Machine Learning (ML)

 └── Neural Networks (Deep Learning)

Understanding this relationship helps you clearly talk about AI, ML, or neural networks depending on the context.

🪣 Common Misunderstandings Clarified

- **Myth:** AI, ML, and Neural Networks mean the same thing.

  - **Truth:** AI is the broad concept; ML is one of its main methods; Neural Networks are a specialized ML technique.

- **Myth:** Neural Networks mimic exactly how human brains think.

  - **Truth:** They're inspired by brain structure, but don't replicate true human thought or emotion.

- **Myth:** ML and AI systems always give correct answers.

- ○ **Truth:** They learn from data. If data has flaws, so will their answers.

📝 Summing It All Up

- **AI:** The overall goal—machines performing human-like tasks intelligently.

- **Machine Learning:** One key AI technique—computers learn patterns directly from data.

- **Neural Networks:** A powerful form of ML that's revolutionized image and speech recognition, translation, and complex predictions.

Clearly knowing these differences helps you choose and use AI tools more effectively. Whether you're just curious or planning to dive deeper, clarity makes AI far less intimidating and much more useful.

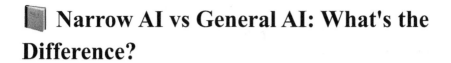 Narrow AI vs General AI: What's the Difference?

When people talk about Artificial Intelligence, they often think of machines that can do everything humans can—learn anything, solve any problem, even experience emotions. But in reality, AI today is far more limited. Understanding the difference between **Narrow AI** and **General AI** will help you clearly see what AI can achieve now—and what's still science fiction.

Simply put:

- **Narrow AI (also known as "weak AI")** refers to AI designed to do specific tasks extremely well, like recognizing your voice or recommending music.

- **General AI (also called "strong AI")** describes machines that can think, reason, and learn exactly like humans, handling any intellectual task you give them.

Right now, all real-world AI falls into the "Narrow AI" category. General AI remains a theoretical goal scientists have not yet achieved—but continue striving toward.

Let's explore clearly what separates these two ideas, why the distinction matters, and what it means for our future.

🎯 Narrow AI: Specialized Intelligence

When you use Alexa to play music or ask Google Maps for directions, you're experiencing Narrow AI. It's called "narrow" because each AI system is designed and trained specifically to do one task—or a small set of tasks—extremely well. It doesn't actually "understand" in a human sense. It simply analyzes data, recognizes patterns, and makes decisions based on what it's learned.

Think of Narrow AI as specialized experts. Just as a skilled mechanic specializes in car repair or a dentist knows everything about teeth, Narrow AI systems specialize in tasks like translating languages, sorting emails, or identifying people from photographs.

Examples of Narrow AI	What They Specialize In
Netflix Recommendations	Predicting shows or movies you'll enjoy
Google Translate	Translating languages quickly
Siri or Alexa	Understanding spoken commands and answering clearly
Email Spam Filters	Detecting unwanted emails
Facial Recognition	Identifying faces accurately

Why Narrow AI works well:

- It can be trained efficiently with clear goals and structured data.

- It requires fewer resources compared to broader, human-like intelligence.

- It excels at repetitive or clearly defined tasks, often faster and more accurately than humans.

But Narrow AI has its limits. Ask your GPS to recommend a movie or your Netflix app to check the weather, and you'll quickly see how specialized—and limited—each system is. They excel only within their narrow areas of expertise.

🌐 General AI: Human-Like Intelligence (Still a Dream)

General AI is the ambitious goal of creating AI that matches or surpasses human intelligence in every way— thinking, reasoning, solving problems across diverse topics, and adapting quickly to new situations. Imagine an AI that can cook dinner, write poetry, drive a car, discuss philosophy, and comfort you when you're feeling down— all equally well. This is what General AI promises.

Unlike Narrow AI, General AI wouldn't need to be specifically trained for each new task. Instead, it would independently learn, reason, and adapt much like a human brain does. It would use broad intelligence and common sense to handle any challenge thrown its way.

Yet General AI remains purely theoretical. We simply don't yet know how to recreate the complex, flexible thinking that humans do effortlessly every day.

General AI capabilities (theoretical):

✅ Solve new problems without specific training

✅ Learn quickly from minimal information

✅ Adapt instantly to unfamiliar situations

✅ Understand context, humor, and nuance

✅ Express empathy and creativity

As exciting as General AI sounds, achieving it faces massive hurdles. Scientists aren't yet sure how to build machines capable of human-like reasoning, creativity, and genuine understanding. Some experts believe it's decades away—or may never be fully possible.

⚖️ Why Does This Distinction Matter?

Knowing the difference between Narrow AI and General AI matters for several practical reasons:

- **Realistic Expectations:**
  Understanding Narrow AI's limits helps avoid unrealistic fears or hopes about what AI can do today.

- **Ethical Implications:**
  The possibility of General AI raises important questions about ethics, responsibility, and the future of humanity itself. Should we build machines that can think just like humans? If we do, how do we ensure they remain helpful rather than harmful?

- **Career and Education Choices:**
  Knowing Narrow AI dominates today can guide decisions about which skills to learn or what career paths to pursue. Right now, careers focusing on managing, developing, or working alongside specialized AI are booming.

Clearly recognizing where we stand today (Narrow AI) and what remains hypothetical (General AI) is crucial for practical decision-making in your daily life, work, and future planning.

▶ Common Misconceptions About General AI

Let's clear up some common myths about General AI:

- **Myth:** General AI already exists (or will appear very soon).
  Reality: We currently have no real-world examples

of General AI. Experts believe it's still decades away, if achievable at all.

- **Myth:** Narrow AI will naturally evolve into General AI on its own.
  Reality: Narrow AI requires specific training for every task. Achieving General AI will require fundamental scientific breakthroughs, not just incremental progress.

- **Myth:** Once General AI arrives, it will automatically mean a utopian (or dystopian) future.
  Reality: How General AI is developed and used will depend entirely on human choices, ethics, and careful control.

Looking to the Future: What's Next?

Researchers around the world continue striving toward General AI, driven by curiosity and ambition. But the more immediate—and realistic—future involves Narrow AI becoming even smarter, more efficient, and deeply integrated into our lives.

In the next few years, expect Narrow AI to expand into more industries, making tasks simpler, faster, and more automated. But always remember—these AI tools will remain highly specialized, not truly human-like. Any move toward General AI will come slowly, step-by-step, with plenty of ethical debate and oversight.

📖 Summing It All Up Clearly

- **Narrow AI:** Specialized intelligence performing single tasks exceptionally well. This is the AI you interact with daily (like Siri, Netflix recommendations, and self-driving cars).

- **General AI:** Broad, flexible intelligence equal to human intelligence, currently theoretical and still far beyond our present capabilities.

Understanding this clear distinction lets you use and discuss AI confidently, realistically, and responsibly.

📘 Common Myths About AI (And What's Actually True)

Artificial Intelligence (AI) is everywhere these days—in your phone, your car, even your bank account. But as AI grows more common, myths and misunderstandings also spread quickly. Separating truth from fiction about AI is important because it shapes how we use, trust, and prepare for this powerful technology.

Let's clearly examine some of the most common myths about AI, explain what's actually true, and help you see AI realistically—without hype or fear.

► Myth 1: "AI Will Soon Take Over All Human Jobs"

Reality: AI is definitely changing jobs, but it isn't replacing all human workers—at least not anytime soon. Instead, AI typically automates repetitive or predictable tasks, leaving humans more time for creative, strategic, or complex work.

For example, automated checkouts in stores replace some cashier roles. But humans are still needed for customer service, handling unusual requests, and overseeing technology. In healthcare, AI helps doctors by diagnosing illnesses faster, but doctors themselves aren't going away —instead, they focus more on patient care and decision-making.

Jobs AI Will Likely Change or Replace	Jobs AI Will Enhance or Create
✓ Cashiers (self-checkouts)	✓ Healthcare professionals (AI-assisted diagnosis)
✓ Telemarketers (automated calls)	✓ Teachers (personalized AI learning tools)
✓ Data-entry clerks (automation)	✓ Writers & Creators (AI tools for inspiration)

Bottom line: AI reshapes jobs rather than fully replacing them, creating both challenges and opportunities.

▶ Myth 2: "AI Systems Are Always Neutral and Fair"

Reality: AI systems learn from human data, which means they can inherit human biases. For example, if a hiring AI studies past employee data, it might unintentionally discriminate against certain groups if historical hiring practices were unfair.

A famous case involved an AI hiring tool that favored male applicants simply because most historical hires in that role were men. Once discovered, this bias had to be actively corrected.

The lesson: AI itself isn't inherently biased, but its decisions can reflect human bias from the data it learns from. Ensuring fairness requires actively monitoring AI systems and carefully selecting training data.

▶ Myth 3: "AI Can Understand and Experience Human Emotions"

Reality: AI might seem emotional at times—like when a chatbot comforts you or expresses sympathy. But this is just clever programming and learned responses. AI doesn't feel happiness, sadness, or empathy in the human sense.

Consider a customer support chatbot saying, "I understand your frustration." It isn't genuinely empathizing; it's simply responding based on data patterns it learned to recognize. True emotional understanding requires experiences and self-awareness—something AI currently doesn't have.

Simple comparison:

What AI Can Do	What AI Can't Actually Do
✓ Recognize and mimic emotions based on data	✗ Truly feel emotions (happiness, sadness)
✓ Provide comfort using learned phrases	✗ Have genuine emotional awareness

▶ Myth 4: "AI Systems Always Get It Right"

Reality: AI systems learn from patterns and data, but they're not perfect. Mistakes happen—sometimes often. For instance, facial recognition AI can occasionally misidentify people, navigation systems might send you on unusual routes, and even advanced chatbots can give incorrect or misleading answers.

AI accuracy depends heavily on:

- **Quality and quantity of training data:** Bad data equals bad decisions.

- **Complexity of the task:** Simpler tasks (like sorting spam emails) are usually more accurate than complex tasks (like fully autonomous driving).

Remember: AI is helpful but fallible. Always verify critical AI decisions rather than relying entirely on automated systems.

▶ Myth 5: "AI Will Automatically Become Dangerous or Evil"

Reality: AI systems are tools created by humans, controlled by their programming and purpose. They don't become "evil" or "dangerous" on their own. However, AI can become harmful if used irresponsibly, carelessly, or maliciously by people.

For instance, AI can be misused to create realistic fake videos ("deepfakes"), deceive people, or spread misinformation online. But it's humans—not AI itself—that determine how these tools are used.

Responsible AI Use	Irresponsible AI Use
✓ Healthcare (diagnosis, patient care)	✗ Creating deepfake videos to spread false news
✓ Traffic Management (safer roads)	✗ Facial recognition used without consent

Clearly put: AI is as safe or dangerous as the humans designing, deploying, and using it.

► Myth 6: "AI Is Intelligent Just Like Humans"

Reality: AI intelligence isn't human intelligence. Humans think broadly, creatively, and flexibly. AI, on the other hand, excels at specific tasks when given clear data and instructions but lacks true understanding or imagination.

For instance, an AI can quickly solve math problems, recognize millions of faces, or translate languages. But it can't independently understand why those tasks matter or creatively decide new goals without human guidance.

Human Intelligence	AI Intelligence
✔ Thinks creatively, flexibly	✔ Excels at specialized, data-driven tasks
✔ Learns from diverse experiences	✔ Learns from specific datasets
✔ Understands context deeply	✔ Limited contextual understanding

Conclusion: AI complements human intelligence; it doesn't replace it fully.

► Myth 7: "AI Will Naturally Become Super-Intelligent and Out of Control"

Reality: AI doesn't spontaneously evolve into something uncontrollable. It improves incrementally through deliberate human decisions, programming, and adjustments. There's no magical leap from narrow, specialized AI to powerful, autonomous "super-intelligence."

While many experts discuss the potential risks of highly advanced AI, any real-world advances happen slowly, step-by-step, and remain fully under human guidance and supervision.

Important clarification:

- **Realistic scenario:** Gradual, carefully managed improvements in AI.

- **Science fiction scenario:** Sudden, uncontrollable AI evolution without human oversight.

🔑 Why Debunking Myths Matters

Clearing up misconceptions matters for several important reasons:

- **Better Decisions:** Understanding what AI can and can't do helps you choose and use AI tools wisely.

- **Realistic Expectations:** Avoiding unrealistic fears or expectations about AI's abilities helps you prepare for real-world opportunities and challenges.

- **Responsible Development:** Recognizing AI limitations guides responsible AI design and use.

📝 Summing It All Up Clearly

Myths about AI spread quickly, but separating truth from fiction gives you clarity and confidence. AI is neither all-powerful nor dangerously uncontrollable. It's a useful, specialized, fallible tool made by and guided by humans. Understanding these truths lets you benefit from AI's strengths without fearing unrealistic threats.

📔 Why AI Matters Today — In Your Life and Work

Artificial Intelligence might sound futuristic—something distant, technical, and complicated. But the truth is simpler and much closer to home. AI matters right now because it's quietly woven into your everyday life and profoundly affects your work, leisure, health, and family activities—even if you don't always notice it.

Clearly understanding AI's impact today helps you leverage it effectively, stay ahead in your career, simplify daily tasks, and improve your overall quality of life. Let's explore exactly why AI matters so much right now, breaking it down into clear, practical ways it already helps you daily and will continue shaping your future.

🏠 AI in Your Daily Routine

AI is already embedded deeply in your day-to-day activities—making tasks quicker, easier, and more efficient. Here's a typical morning scenario:

- Your alarm gently wakes you at just the right moment, detecting your sleep pattern (AI in health and fitness apps).

- Alexa or Siri summarizes today's weather and news, clearly answering your questions and preparing you for the day.

- You quickly ask your smart assistant to adjust your home's thermostat or lights, making your environment comfortable before you get out of bed.

Throughout your day, AI keeps helping:

Routine Task	How AI Makes It Easier
Shopping & Recommendations	AI suggests products you might like based on your past preferences (Amazon, Netflix).
Navigation & Traffic	AI finds the quickest route, helping you avoid traffic jams (Google Maps, Waze).
Managing Your Schedule	AI automatically sets reminders, meetings, or appointments (Google Assistant, Siri).

AI matters because it saves you time, effort, and frustration—automating repetitive tasks and freeing your mind for more important things.

AI's Impact on Your Work

No matter your profession, AI is already reshaping how you work—boosting productivity, accuracy, and efficiency. Consider the following examples clearly demonstrating AI's practical value across different job roles:

- **Office Workers:**
  AI automatically sorts emails, schedules meetings, and summarizes key points from lengthy documents or calls, saving hours weekly.

- **Marketers & Salespeople:**
  AI identifies the best customers to target, personalizes ads, or automatically manages customer interactions, significantly boosting sales.

- **Healthcare Professionals:**
  AI tools quickly analyze patient data to detect

illnesses, recommend treatments, and help manage patient records more accurately.

- **Teachers & Educators:**
  AI personalizes learning experiences, instantly grades tests, or flags students needing extra attention, improving educational outcomes.

Clearly put, AI doesn't replace your job—it enhances it, giving you more time and tools to focus on creativity, strategy, and critical thinking.

AI in Your Finances

AI is quietly transforming your financial life, helping you manage money more effectively and securely:

- **Budgeting and Saving:**
  AI apps analyze your spending patterns and suggest easy ways to save money. Apps like Mint or YNAB use AI to identify wasteful spending and suggest realistic budgets.

- **Investing:**
  AI-powered tools like robo-advisors automatically build diversified investment portfolios tailored to your goals, reducing stress about financial decisions.

- **Fraud Detection:**
  AI constantly monitors your bank accounts or credit cards, instantly alerting you about unusual activity to keep your finances safe.

AI Financial Tool	Practical Benefit
Mint, YNAB, EveryDollar	Budget smarter by clearly tracking expenses
Wealthfront, Betterment	Automated, stress-free investing strategies
Credit Card Alerts	Instant detection of suspicious transactions

AI for Your Health and Wellness

AI matters greatly for health because it helps you maintain well-being and detect issues earlier:

- **Fitness Apps & Wearables:**
  AI-powered devices like Fitbit, Apple Watch, or Garmin analyze your sleep patterns, exercise habits, heart rate, and stress levels, clearly giving personalized recommendations for improved health.

- **Nutrition Guidance:**
  AI-driven apps analyze your eating habits and suggest personalized meal plans or diets to meet your goals, such as losing weight or building muscle.

- **Mental Health Support:**
  Apps powered by AI provide affordable, personalized mental health support, helping manage stress, anxiety, or depression anytime you need it.

Health App or Device	AI's Role in Your Wellness
Fitbit, Apple Health	Monitors your fitness, sleep, and heart health
MyFitnessPal, Lose It!	Personalized meal tracking and dietary advice
Woebot, Calm, Headspace	Instant mental health and stress-relief support

 AI and Learning: Education for Everyone

AI matters deeply in education, making it more accessible, personalized, and effective for learners of every age:

- **Personalized Learning:**
  AI adapts to your unique strengths and weaknesses, providing lessons customized exactly to your learning style and pace (Duolingo, Khan Academy).

- **Instant Feedback & Assistance:**
  AI-powered tutors instantly answer questions, clarify confusing topics, and offer continuous support, greatly improving learning efficiency.

- **Inclusive Education:**
  AI helps students with disabilities by providing specialized learning tools, transcription, or real-time translations, making education more accessible than ever.

AI-Powered Education Tools	Clear Benefits to Learners
Duolingo, Babbel	Quickly learn new languages
Khan Academy, Coursera	Personalized education at your own pace
Grammarly, Hemingway	Instant grammar, style, and writing assistance

 **AI in Relationships & Family Life**

Even personal and family relationships can benefit from AI, making life easier and more enjoyable:

- **Parenting Support:**
  AI-powered devices and apps help manage family schedules, educational activities for kids, and even offer advice for parenting challenges.

- **Staying Connected:**
  Video calls enhanced by AI (Zoom, Google Meet) keep distant family and friends connected clearly, even optimizing poor internet connections.

Family AI Applications	Real-Life Use
Google Family Link, Life360	Track family location and safety instantly
Alexa, Siri at Home	Family scheduling, entertainment, and information
Photo Apps (Google Photos)	Automatically organizes family memories clearly

Why Understanding AI's Impact Matters Now

AI's growing presence matters deeply for your future. Clearly understanding its practical benefits—and limitations—gives you a huge advantage:

- **Career Opportunities:**
  Understanding AI helps you stay relevant professionally, increasing job security and opening new career paths.

- **Daily Efficiency:**
  AI simplifies routines, freeing you to spend more

quality time on what truly matters—family, hobbies, creativity.

- **Personal Well-being:**
  AI improves health, learning, and relationships, clearly contributing to a happier, healthier life overall.

AI isn't just another passing trend. It's reshaping daily life in tangible, beneficial ways that truly matter.

📘 How AI "Thinks": Simple Logic Behind the Code

When people say Artificial Intelligence "thinks," it can sound like magic or even a little intimidating. How exactly does a computer decide, predict, or recognize things the way humans do? The good news is, AI doesn't actually think or feel like a human—it simply follows clear, logical rules and learns from patterns in data.

Let's break down clearly how AI makes decisions step-by-step, without complicated jargon or technical overload. Understanding how AI "thinks" makes it less mysterious and more useful in your daily life.

🧩 AI's Simple Logic: Patterns and Predictions

At the simplest level, AI learns by looking at examples and finding patterns. Imagine teaching a child to recognize dogs. You'd show the child many dogs—small dogs, big dogs, different breeds—until the child learns key features (four legs, tail, ears, fur). Once they've seen enough examples, the child quickly identifies any new dog they encounter.

AI works similarly. It examines large amounts of data, learns patterns, and uses these patterns to make predictions or decisions. This process—called **machine learning**—forms the heart of AI's logical "thinking."

Here's how it works clearly in practice:

1 **Input data (examples)**: AI first examines thousands of images of dogs, labeled correctly as "dog."

2   **Finding patterns**: AI identifies features dogs usually share (fur, tails, shape, size).

3   **Learning process**: AI remembers these patterns as rules for identifying dogs.

4   **Prediction or decision**: When you show a new image, AI checks it against these learned patterns and decides, "This is likely a dog."

Simple, logical, and effective. No magic—just clear rules learned through repeated examples.

◎ Real-life Example: How AI Recognizes Your Voice

When you say, "Hey Siri," your phone instantly responds. How does AI do that? Let's clearly break down how AI "thinks" when recognizing your voice:

- **Step 1: Capturing the sound**
  Your voice command ("Hey Siri, what's the weather?") is turned into digital signals your phone can analyze.

- **Step 2: Recognizing words**
  AI compares the digital signals to patterns it's learned from millions of voice examples, quickly identifying the words you're speaking.

- **Step 3: Understanding meaning**
  AI recognizes key phrases ("weather," "today"), clearly identifying your request and deciding what you want.

- **Step 4: Gathering information**
  AI automatically retrieves current weather data from online sources.

- **Step 5: Providing the answer**
  Finally, AI converts the information into clear, spoken sentences like, "Today will be sunny and 75 degrees."

In each step, AI logically matches patterns from data (sounds, words, phrases) to reach a clear, accurate decision. There's no guessing—just carefully learned patterns and logic.

⚙ How AI Learns

To clearly understand how AI thinks, let's simplify the learning process into three straightforward methods:

1. Supervised Learning (Learning from Examples):
Like learning from flashcards. AI receives clearly labeled examples—like images labeled "cat" or "dog"—and uses them to recognize future images.

Input (Examples)	AI's Logic	Output (Decision)
Image labeled "dog"	Learns key features of a dog (tail, fur)	Recognizes new dogs instantly
Email labeled "spam"	Learns spam patterns (phrases, senders)	Filters out future spam

2. Unsupervised Learning (Learning from Patterns):
AI finds hidden patterns by itself. Imagine grouping similar objects without labels—AI spots similarities, organizing data logically without human guidance.

Example:

- AI organizes customer behavior into clear groups, helping businesses target products more effectively.

3. Reinforcement Learning (Learning from Feedback):
Similar to training a pet. AI tries different actions, receives feedback (rewards or penalties), and gradually learns the best action for each situation.

Example:

- AI learns how to win chess games by trying moves, seeing outcomes, and remembering successful strategies.

📌 **Simple Example: AI Decision Logic (Shopping Recommendations)**

You've noticed Amazon recommends products surprisingly well. How does AI logically "think" to make these suggestions?

- **Step 1:** AI analyzes your past behavior (products you viewed, bought, or liked).

- **Step 2:** It compares your choices to thousands of other customers who made similar choices.

- **Step 3:** It logically predicts products you're likely to enjoy based on these patterns.

- **Step 4:** Amazon clearly displays personalized suggestions.

No guesswork involved—just clear, logical patterns.

► Common Misunderstandings Clarified

Here's what AI doesn't do when it "thinks":

- ✖ **Doesn't guess randomly.** AI always bases decisions on learned data patterns.

- ✖ **Doesn't truly "understand" context or emotions.** AI decisions rely on logic and data—not true empathy or understanding.

- ✖ **Doesn't learn instantly.** AI needs many examples and careful training to learn accurately.

🔍 AI's Logic Clearly Explained (In One Table)

AI Task	Input (Data examples)	AI's Logical Thinking	Output (Decision)
Voice Recognition	Your spoken commands	Matches speech patterns	Clearly responds to commands
Email Sorting	Past emails labeled as spam or not spam	Identifies common spam patterns	Accurately filters emails
Driving (Autonomous Cars)	Images/videos of roads, cars, pedestrians	Recognizes objects and follows clear safety rules	Makes safe driving decisions

This table clearly shows AI's logical, step-by-step process —no magic or guesswork.

Why Understanding AI's Logic Matters to You

Clearly understanding how AI thinks matters for several reasons:

- **Confidence & Trust:** Knowing AI's logic helps you trust its decisions.

- **Smarter Use:** You use AI tools better by understanding their limits.

- **Career Advantage:** Clearly knowing how AI learns gives you a professional advantage in an increasingly AI-driven world.

What AI Can and Can't Do (For Now)

Artificial Intelligence (AI) often feels powerful, almost magical—helping you find directions, recommending new shows, even answering complex questions instantly. But AI also has clear limits. Understanding exactly what AI **can** and **can't** do right now matters, because realistic expectations help you confidently use AI without frustration or disappointment.

Let's clearly explore what AI excels at today, along with tasks it still struggles with—so you know exactly what to expect in your daily life, work, and beyond.

What AI Can Do Well (Today)

Right now, AI is excellent at tasks involving clear patterns, vast amounts of data, and straightforward logic. Here are some clear examples of areas where AI shines today:

- **Pattern Recognition:** AI excels at recognizing patterns—faces, voices, handwriting, and more. Your smartphone uses AI to instantly recognize your face, unlocking the screen without delay. Social media apps use AI to recognize friends in photos.

- **Repetitive Tasks:** AI easily handles routine or repetitive tasks like sorting emails, tracking expenses, or suggesting Netflix shows you might like based on your previous viewing history.

- **Quick Decision-Making from Data:** AI quickly analyzes large data sets to make predictions. Banks use AI to detect fraud by recognizing unusual spending patterns instantly, protecting your finances.

- **Language Translation & Understanding:** AI clearly translates languages in real-time. Google Translate or apps like Duolingo instantly interpret words and sentences, allowing easy communication across languages.

Here's a clear summary of AI's strongest current abilities:

AI Strengths (Today)	Practical Examples
Pattern Recognition	Face recognition, fingerprint unlocking
Repetitive Task Automation	Spam filtering, email organization
Instant Data Analysis	Fraud detection, traffic navigation
Language Understanding	Google Translate, voice assistants (Alexa, Siri)

Clearly, AI is highly effective at specialized tasks involving data patterns, logic, and well-defined processes.

🚧 What AI Still Can't Do Well (Yet)

Despite its strengths, AI still faces clear limitations—especially tasks requiring human-like understanding, creativity, empathy, or context-awareness. Here's exactly where AI falls short today:

- **Truly Understanding Context:**
  AI struggles to understand subtle human contexts or nuances. A joke or sarcastic comment often confuses AI systems because they interpret everything literally, based solely on data patterns, not emotional or situational context.

- **Creativity and Originality:**
  While AI can create music, stories, or art by mimicking patterns from data, it can't truly imagine new concepts independently. Its creativity comes from combining existing data patterns—not genuine imagination or originality.

- **Complex Emotional and Social Interaction:**
  AI doesn't genuinely understand human emotions. While AI can respond to emotional expressions ("I'm sad") by following programmed patterns, it doesn't experience or empathize emotionally the way people do.

- **Instantly Adapting to Unexpected Situations:**
  AI learns from past data. In completely new, unexpected scenarios where no similar data exists, AI struggles greatly. Humans quickly adapt using intuition; AI needs clear, familiar examples first.

AI Weaknesses (Today)	Practical Examples of Limitations
Context & Nuance	Misinterpreting sarcasm, humor, or subtle meanings
Genuine Creativity & Imagination	Unable to create truly original ideas independently
Emotional Understanding	No real empathy or deep emotional connection
Adaptability to Unknown Situations	Struggles without familiar data or clear guidelines

Clearly put, AI today remains limited compared to flexible, intuitive human thinking.

🎯 Practical Examples: What AI Can vs. Can't Do

Let's look clearly at practical examples comparing tasks AI handles well to those it still can't perform effectively:

Situation	✅ AI Can	🚫 AI Can't (Yet)
Chatting Online	Answer simple questions quickly and clearly	Fully understand emotional or subtle conversations
Driving Cars	Navigate highways under clear conditions	Safely drive under all complex, unexpected conditions
Financial Decisions	Detect fraud from spending patterns	Make complex ethical financial decisions
Medical Diagnosis	Quickly analyze X-rays or scans	Comfort and emotionally reassure patients
Creative Projects (Art)	Generate art based on learned patterns	Independently imagine groundbreaking artistic concepts

Understanding these clear examples helps you realistically gauge when and how to rely on AI in your daily life and career.

▶ Common Misunderstandings Clarified

Let's clearly correct some common misconceptions about AI capabilities:

- **Myth:** AI can solve any problem if you feed it enough data.
  Reality: AI solves specific, clearly defined problems well, but struggles greatly with ambiguous, emotional, or creative tasks, regardless of data.

- **Myth:** AI always improves automatically with time.
  Reality: AI improves only when humans clearly feed it high-quality data and carefully update its logic. It doesn't magically get smarter independently.

- **Myth:** AI's creativity matches or surpasses humans.
  Reality: AI creativity is limited to remixing learned patterns, not genuine originality or imagination.

🧭 What Does This Mean for Your Future?

Clearly understanding AI's current capabilities and limitations prepares you for a realistic future:

- **Career Opportunities:**
  Jobs involving clear logic, data analysis, and routine tasks are becoming AI-driven. Careers requiring creativity, emotional intelligence, and adaptability remain human strengths.

- **Daily Life & Decision-Making:**
  Rely on AI for clearly defined tasks (navigation, translations, recommendations), but stay skeptical or cautious about AI's decisions on complex emotional or moral issues.

- **Skill Development:**
  Develop your uniquely human strengths (creativity, emotional intelligence, adaptability), making you more valuable in an AI-enhanced future.

Summing It All Up Clearly

Artificial Intelligence today is powerful but specialized. AI excels at pattern recognition, repetitive tasks, data-driven decisions, and language translation. Yet it struggles with genuine creativity, emotional empathy, understanding nuanced context, and adapting quickly to completely new situations.

Clearly understanding these differences helps you use AI effectively and confidently, without unrealistic expectations.

SECTION 2

AI IN YOUR DAILY LIFE

(Practical uses of AI at home, for health, learning & routine tasks)

AI for Everyday Tasks: Schedules, Shopping, Planning

Artificial Intelligence (AI) isn't something limited to science labs or big tech companies anymore—it's quietly helping you every day. In fact, AI is probably making your life easier right now, even if you're not fully aware of it. Whether you're planning your day, shopping online, or managing your family's busy schedules, AI tools simplify your routine tasks, saving you valuable time and mental energy.

In this chapter, we'll explore clearly how AI helps manage your daily tasks, schedule efficiently, shop smarter, and plan effortlessly. You'll learn exactly how to benefit from these powerful but easy-to-use AI tools in practical ways, without any tech overwhelm.

AI for Scheduling and Time Management

Most of us juggle busy schedules, meetings, family events, and daily responsibilities. Keeping everything straight can feel overwhelming. That's where AI comes in —making managing your calendar easy, quick, and stress-free.

How does AI scheduling work?
AI apps analyze your calendar, tasks, and preferences, then automatically suggest optimal times for appointments, meetings, or daily activities. No more endless back-and-forth emails or forgetting important events.

Here's exactly how AI simplifies your scheduling:

- **Smart Scheduling (Google Calendar, Outlook):** AI automatically finds open slots in your schedule and suggests meeting times, considering availability, location, and even travel times.

- **Intelligent Reminders (Siri, Google Assistant):** AI reminds you about tasks based on your habits, preferences, or location—like reminding you to buy milk when passing a grocery store.

Clear example:

"Hey Siri, schedule a dentist appointment next Tuesday morning."
AI instantly checks your calendar and finds the best available time, clearly confirming the appointment without extra effort.

AI Scheduling Tool	Clear Benefit for You
Google Calendar	Automatically manages meetings, travel times
Calendly, Clara	Sets up meetings instantly without emails
Siri, Google Assistant	Quickly schedules tasks by voice commands

Simply put, AI scheduling takes away stress, freeing you to focus clearly on what truly matters in your day.

AI in Shopping: Easier, Faster, Smarter

Shopping with AI saves you time, money, and frustration by suggesting products you'll genuinely enjoy, finding deals instantly, and automating routine purchases clearly and efficiently.

Personalized Recommendations:
AI learns your preferences and shopping history, clearly recommending products you'll likely love. For instance, Amazon suggests products based on your previous purchases and browsing habits, making shopping faster and simpler.

Price Tracking and Deals:
AI-powered apps (like Honey or CamelCamelCamel) automatically track product prices and clearly alert you when items you want drop in price, saving you money without extra effort.

Routine Purchases Simplified:
AI can automatically reorder household essentials like detergent, paper towels, or groceries—clearly simplifying your weekly shopping.

AI Shopping Tools	Clear Benefits for Your Life
Amazon Recommendations	Instantly suggests products you actually want
Honey, Rakuten	Automatically finds the best coupons or deals
Instacart, Walmart Grocery	Automates grocery shopping based on your regular purchases

A practical scenario of AI shopping:

You run low on toothpaste. Amazon's AI instantly suggests your usual brand at the best price, and it arrives automatically at your door before you run out—no extra thinking required.

AI in Daily Planning and Task Management

Every day involves multiple tasks and decisions. AI helps you clearly organize and prioritize these tasks, ensuring you remain productive without feeling overwhelmed.

AI-Powered To-Do Lists (Todoist, Microsoft To Do):
AI prioritizes your tasks automatically based on deadlines, importance, and your past habits. It suggests clearly what you should focus on first, removing decision fatigue from your daily planning.

Smart Assistants (Alexa, Siri):
AI helps you quickly create lists by voice ("Alexa, add eggs to my shopping list"), then reminds you exactly when you need those items.

Practical Example of AI Daily Planning:

- AI notices you typically shop on weekends, reminding you clearly on Friday evening about your weekend grocery list, preventing forgotten items or last-minute stress.

AI Task Management Tools	Clear Benefits for Your Daily Routine
Todoist, Microsoft To Do	Clearly prioritize daily tasks effortlessly
Evernote, Notion AI	Automatically organize notes and ideas
Alexa Shopping Lists	Quickly manage lists hands-free

▶ Common Misunderstandings Clarified

Clearly understand what AI can—and can't—do for your daily tasks:

- ❌ **Myth:** AI will always know exactly what you want without you saying anything.

  ✅ **Reality:** AI learns from your habits, but still clearly benefits from your input to improve recommendations.

- ❌ **Myth:** AI planning completely removes human decision-making.

  ✅ **Reality:** AI suggests and simplifies tasks, but you remain fully in control of the final decisions and priorities.

📌 AI Everyday Task Checklist

Clearly benefit from AI tools by regularly using these practical tips in your daily life:

- ✅ Let AI automatically manage scheduling to avoid stress or conflicts.

- ✅ Use AI shopping assistants to save money and time.

- ✅ Allow AI-powered task lists to clearly prioritize your daily activities.

📝 Summing It All Up Clearly

Artificial Intelligence already significantly simplifies your daily routine—organizing schedules, suggesting products you love, managing daily tasks, and helping you plan effectively. Clearly leveraging these practical AI tools makes everyday tasks quicker, easier, and stress-free.

Understanding exactly how AI supports you every day gives you more time and energy for what truly matters—family, relaxation, creativity, and enjoying life.

🔘 Voice Assistants: Alexa, Google, Siri – What They Really Do

Voice assistants like Alexa, Google Assistant, and Siri have quickly become part of our daily routines. You've probably used them yourself—asking questions, playing music, or even setting reminders hands-free. But do you really know exactly what these assistants can (and can't) do?

Clearly understanding the real power behind voice assistants helps you maximize their usefulness in your everyday life—saving time, simplifying routines, and making tasks easier. Let's dive deeper into how Alexa, Google Assistant, and Siri truly work, what practical benefits they offer, and where they still fall short.

🎙️ How Voice Assistants Actually Work (Simply Explained)

At first glance, voice assistants might seem almost magical: you ask a question out loud, and you instantly receive a clear, accurate answer. But there's simple, logical technology behind how they work. Here's exactly how voice assistants handle your commands clearly and quickly:

1. **Listening & Converting Speech to Text:**
   When you say, "Hey Siri" or "Alexa," the device clearly captures your voice and converts the spoken words into digital text.

2. **Understanding Your Request (Natural Language Processing):**
   AI analyzes your text to clearly understand what

you're asking. It identifies key words and phrases, determining exactly what action to perform or information to find.

3   **Finding the Answer:**
Once AI knows what you need, it instantly searches the internet or your connected services (calendars, smart home devices, apps) to find the correct information.

4   **Speaking Clearly Back to You:**
Finally, the AI converts the answer into clear spoken words, delivering it back through your device's speakers within seconds.

Here's a simple example clearly showing this process in action:

You: "Alexa, what's today's weather?"
Alexa:

1   Captures your voice, turning it into digital text.

2   Understands you're asking about current weather conditions.

3   Retrieves weather data from an online service.

4   Clearly replies, "Today it's sunny, with a high of 75 degrees."

📌 Practical Things Voice Assistants Really Do Well

Voice assistants excel at clear, straightforward tasks, saving you significant time and effort. Here are everyday examples of exactly how they practically help:

- **Quick Information and Answers:**
  Instantly providing clear, helpful answers ("What's the capital of Spain?", "Convert 5 cups to ounces.") without needing to open apps or search manually.

- **Daily Scheduling and Reminders:**
  Clearly scheduling appointments ("Set a dentist appointment for Tuesday at 10 AM") or reminding you about tasks ("Remind me to call Mom tonight").

- **Hands-Free Communication:**
  Making calls or sending messages ("Text Sarah I'll be late") safely, even while driving or cooking.

- **Entertainment:**
  Easily controlling your music, podcasts, or audiobooks with simple voice commands ("Play my workout playlist on Spotify").

Voice Assistant Task	Clear Practical Benefit for You
Information and Questions	Quick answers without manual searches
Daily Reminders and Alarms	Clearly manages your daily tasks automatically
Communication	Safely handles calls and texts hands-free
Smart Home Control	Effortlessly controls lighting, temperature, and appliances

Simply put, voice assistants remove friction from routine tasks, making everyday life easier.

🚧 What Voice Assistants Still Struggle With

Despite being incredibly useful, voice assistants clearly have limitations. Recognizing these helps set realistic expectations:

- **Context and Nuance:**
  Voice assistants often struggle clearly understanding sarcasm, humor, or subtle context. For example, asking Siri, "Is it cold enough to need a jacket?" might confuse it because it interprets commands literally.

- **Complex Requests:**
  Complicated, multi-step commands can be challenging. Clearly stated single-step commands ("Turn off the lights") are easier than long, complex instructions ("Turn off the lights downstairs, lock the front door, and start my coffee maker").

- **Privacy Concerns:**
  Many users worry about privacy because voice assistants are always listening for activation phrases ("Hey Siri"). While they only record after activation, some remain cautious about privacy implications.

Voice Assistant Limitations	Practical Example of Shortcomings
Context & Nuance	Misunderstands humor or sarcasm
Complex Requests	Difficulty handling multi-step or unclear commands
Privacy and Security	Raises concerns about listening devices

Understanding these clear limits helps you use voice assistants effectively without frustration.

🗣 Comparing the Big Three: Alexa, Google Assistant, and Siri

Each voice assistant has clear strengths and weaknesses. Choosing one often depends on your preferences or existing devices:

Feature	Alexa (Amazon)	Google Assistant	Siri (Apple)
Best for Information Searches	Good, but simpler answers	Excellent, detailed responses	Good, but somewhat limited
Smart Home Integration	Excellent smart home control	Good integration (Nest, etc.)	Good, best with Apple HomeKit
Entertainment (Music, Podcasts)	Strong integration with Amazon services	Good, compatible with many services	Good, optimized for Apple Music
Privacy Features	Moderate, voice recordings can be reviewed/deleted	Good, clear privacy controls	Excellent privacy protection

- **Alexa**: Great for smart home control and Amazon services integration.

- **Google Assistant**: Excellent for clear, detailed answers and Android integration.

- **Siri**: Best choice if you prioritize privacy and use mostly Apple products.

▶ Common Misunderstandings Clarified

Here are common myths clearly explained:

- ✖ **Myth:** Voice assistants constantly record everything you say.

  ✅ **Reality:** They only actively listen after hearing the "wake word" (like "Hey Siri" or "Alexa"). However, accidental activations can happen.

- ✖ **Myth:** Voice assistants always give correct answers.

  ✅ **Reality:** They sometimes make mistakes, especially with complex questions or unclear phrasing. Always verify important information.

📝 Summing It All Up Clearly

Voice assistants (Alexa, Google Assistant, Siri) practically enhance your daily life by providing quick information, simplifying communication, managing schedules effortlessly, and controlling smart home devices. Yet they still have clear limitations regarding nuance, complexity, and privacy.

Using voice assistants effectively means clearly knowing their strengths, limitations, and how to leverage them practically for maximum convenience.

⬤ Smart Homes: Lights, Thermostats, and Automation

Imagine waking up in the morning to gently increasing lights, perfect room temperature, and freshly brewed coffee waiting—all without lifting a finger. Smart homes use AI to automate and simplify everyday tasks, transforming your home into a convenient, comfortable, and efficient space tailored exactly to your lifestyle.

In this chapter, we'll clearly explore how AI-powered smart homes work, practical ways they enhance your daily life, and simple steps to get started. You'll see exactly why smart homes matter, how they save you time and money, and the easy ways to set them up—without technical overwhelm.

🏠 What Exactly is a Smart Home? (Clearly Explained)

A "smart home" simply means a home where lights, heating, security systems, appliances, and more connect and interact intelligently—usually through Wi-Fi and AI-driven apps. This connectivity lets you automate and control your home remotely or through simple voice commands, clearly simplifying your daily routine.

Smart homes learn your habits, adjust automatically to your preferences, and can even anticipate your needs. They're convenient, energy-efficient, and save you valuable time—making daily life smoother, safer, and more comfortable.

Here's a clear example of a simple smart home scenario:

You say, "Hey Google, I'm home."
AI instantly:

1   Turns on hallway and living room lights.

2   Adjusts your thermostat to a comfortable
     temperature.

3   Starts playing your favorite music playlist.

No extra effort, just practical, everyday convenience.

Smart Lighting: Convenience and Efficiency

Smart lights offer practical benefits far beyond simple
remote control. They automatically adjust brightness,
color, and even turn themselves off when you leave,
clearly saving energy and money.

Here's exactly how smart lighting practically helps:

- **Automatic Scheduling:**
  Smart lights automatically turn on or off based on
  time, daylight, or even your personal habits. Set
  them to gradually brighten in the morning, helping
  you wake up naturally.

- **Remote and Voice Control:**
  Easily control lights by voice (Alexa, Siri, Google)
  or remotely through an app—no need to get up or
  even be home.

- **Energy Efficiency:**
  Smart lighting detects when rooms are empty,
  automatically turning lights off clearly to save
  electricity and lower your bills.

Smart Lighting Product	Practical Benefits in Daily Life
Philips Hue	Easy automation, voice control, colorful lighting
LIFX Smart Lights	No hub required, app-controlled brightness/colors
Wyze Bulbs	Affordable, clear scheduling and remote control

Clearly put, smart lights simplify daily tasks, enhance comfort, and save money effortlessly.

🔧 Smart Thermostats: Comfort and Cost Savings

Smart thermostats use AI clearly and effectively to manage your home's heating and cooling. They automatically learn your preferred temperatures, adjust schedules based on your routine, and optimize energy use —meaning lower bills and a consistently comfortable home.

Exactly how smart thermostats practically help:

- **Learning Your Preferences:**
  AI quickly learns your preferred temperatures throughout the day and automatically adjusts them —warm in the morning, cooler at night.

- **Automatic Scheduling & Remote Control:**
  Automatically adjusts the temperature based on whether you're home, at work, or on vacation. Control remotely via an app to ensure comfort at all times.

- **Energy Savings:**
  Smart thermostats optimize energy use, clearly

reducing heating and cooling costs by up to 20-30%.

Smart Thermostat	Clear Practical Benefits
Nest Learning Thermostat	Learns quickly, clearly saves energy costs
Ecobee SmartThermostat	Remote sensors optimize room-by-room comfort
Honeywell Home T9	Easy scheduling, clear remote management

A simple example clearly demonstrating benefits:

AI notices you're consistently away from home 9 AM–5 PM weekdays. It automatically lowers your home's heating or cooling during these hours, clearly saving money without sacrificing comfort.

📷 Smart Security & Automation: Safety and Peace of Mind

AI-powered home security systems clearly offer advanced protection, automatically alerting you to unusual activity and ensuring your family's safety:

- **Smart Doorbells & Cameras (Ring, Arlo):**
  Receive instant alerts when someone approaches your door, view live video clearly from anywhere, and easily communicate with visitors remotely.

- **Automated Locks (August, Yale):**
  Lock or unlock doors remotely, provide temporary access clearly for visitors, or ensure doors automatically lock when you leave.

- **Safety Sensors & Alarms (Nest Protect, SimpliSafe):**
  Automatically detect smoke, carbon monoxide, leaks, or intruders, clearly notifying you immediately to keep your home and family safe.

Smart Security Product	Clear Daily Life Benefits
Ring Video Doorbell	Instant video alerts, remote visitor interaction
August Smart Lock	Keyless entry, remote control, temporary guest access
Nest Protect Smoke Detector	Automatic alerts, clearly identifies issues instantly

Clearly put, AI makes home security convenient, reassuring, and instantly effective.

⚙ Easy Steps to Create a Smart Home (Without Tech Overload)

Starting with smart home technology is simpler than you might think. Clearly follow these easy steps:

1 **Pick a Hub or Voice Assistant:**
   Start with Alexa, Google Assistant, or Apple HomeKit to easily control your smart home by voice.

2 **Choose Essential Smart Devices:**
   Clearly start small—lights (Philips Hue), thermostat (Nest), or doorbell camera (Ring). You can always add more devices later.

3 **Connect and Automate:**
   Use easy-to-follow app instructions clearly to set up

and automate your devices, simplifying daily routines quickly.

Example starter pack clearly recommended:

- Voice Assistant (Alexa, Google Home)

- Smart Lights (Philips Hue or LIFX)

- Smart Thermostat (Nest or Ecobee)

- Smart Security (Ring doorbell or August lock)

Within an hour, you'll have a practical, easy-to-use smart home clearly simplifying everyday life.

▶ Common Misunderstandings Clarified

- ✖ **Myth:** Smart homes are too complicated or technical.
  ✅ **Reality:** Setting up smart homes clearly requires no advanced tech knowledge—most systems are simple and clearly guided.

- ✖ **Myth:** Smart homes are always expensive.
  ✅ **Reality:** Many smart home devices are affordable and offer clear energy savings, quickly paying for themselves.

- ✖ **Myth:** Smart home devices invade your privacy.
  ✅ **Reality:** Privacy settings clearly allow you to control exactly what data is collected or shared. Proper settings keep your home secure.

📝 Summing It All Up Clearly

AI-powered smart homes clearly enhance daily comfort, safety, and convenience. Smart lights, thermostats, and security systems automatically simplify tasks, saving time, energy, and money while improving your quality of life.

Creating a smart home is easier than ever—clearly affordable, intuitive, and practically beneficial, allowing you to enjoy life more comfortably and worry-free.

AI for Personal Finance: Budgeting, Saving, Investing

Managing money often feels overwhelming—tracking expenses, balancing budgets, finding ways to save, and figuring out smart investments. Thankfully, AI (Artificial Intelligence) makes handling your personal finances much easier, clearer, and stress-free.

In this chapter, we'll clearly explain how AI practically simplifies budgeting, effortlessly helps you save money, and intelligently guides your investments. You'll learn exactly how to leverage AI-powered financial tools to reduce stress, boost savings, and confidently build financial security.

Budgeting Clearly and Easily with AI

Budgeting is the cornerstone of good financial health. But tracking expenses, categorizing transactions, and staying disciplined is challenging. AI budgeting apps eliminate these headaches by clearly and automatically organizing your finances, showing you exactly where your money goes, and suggesting practical ways to save.

Exactly how AI simplifies budgeting:

- **Automatic Expense Tracking:**
  AI automatically identifies and categorizes expenses clearly from your bank account or credit cards. Apps like Mint or YNAB instantly show spending patterns, highlighting exactly where you overspend or could save more.

- **Personalized Budget Suggestions:**
  AI analyzes your financial habits, clearly recommending realistic, personalized budgets that align exactly with your financial goals.

- **Smart Alerts and Insights:**
  AI proactively notifies you about unusual spending, upcoming bills, or if you're nearing budget limits, clearly keeping your finances on track.

AI Budgeting Tool	Clear Practical Benefit to You
Mint	Automatic tracking, clear spending insights
YNAB (You Need A Budget)	Personalized budget plans, practical saving tips
EveryDollar	Clearly defined budgets, instant alerts

Practical example of AI budgeting:

Mint AI clearly alerts you, "You spent $200 more than usual on dining out this month," helping you quickly adjust your spending before it becomes a problem.

💰 Effortless Saving with AI Tools

Saving money regularly is crucial for financial stability, but it's easy to overlook or put off. AI-powered savings apps simplify saving by clearly and automatically setting aside money without requiring constant effort or discipline from you.

Exactly how AI helps you effortlessly save:

- **Automatic Savings Transfers:**
  Apps like Digit clearly analyze your income, expenses, and habits, then automatically move

small amounts into your savings account regularly—so you save without noticing.

- **Personalized Savings Goals:**
  AI clearly sets personalized, achievable savings targets for emergencies, vacations, or large purchases, making savings practical and motivating.

- **Efficient Bill Management:**
  AI clearly identifies opportunities to lower bills (like subscriptions or utilities) and suggests better options, instantly boosting your savings.

AI Saving Tools	Practical Benefits Clearly Explained
Digit	Automatic transfers, effortless daily savings
Qapital	Customized goals clearly matched to your habits
Truebill (Rocket Money)	Identifies unused subscriptions, clearly saving money

Clear real-life scenario:

Digit clearly identifies you can comfortably save an extra $40 this week and automatically moves it to savings—without any extra effort or stress.

AI for Investing Clearly and Confidently

Investing feels intimidating to many people—often seeming complicated, risky, or confusing. AI-powered investing tools, like robo-advisors, simplify this process by clearly and intelligently managing your investments for you, based on your personal goals and comfort level.

Exactly how AI simplifies investing:

- **Automated Investment Management (Robo-Advisors):**
  AI clearly selects investments tailored to your financial goals (retirement, buying a home, education) and risk tolerance, automatically adjusting your portfolio over time.

- **Instant Diversification and Risk Management:**
  AI instantly creates diversified investment portfolios, clearly minimizing risks while maximizing returns over the long term.

- **Lower Fees and Minimum Investments:**
  Robo-advisors clearly charge lower fees than traditional financial advisors, making professional investing accessible even with smaller amounts of money.

AI Investing Tools	Clear Benefits to Your Financial Future
Wealthfront	Automated portfolios, clear goal-setting tools
Betterment	Simple, transparent investing tailored exactly to your goals
Acorns	Effortlessly invest spare change, clearly growing wealth

Clear example of AI investing:

You deposit $500 into Wealthfront. AI instantly creates a balanced portfolio clearly aligned with your retirement goals, automatically managing your investments without hassle.

▶ Common Misunderstandings Clarified

Clearly correcting myths about AI in personal finance:

- ✖ **Myth:** AI budgeting is complicated or invasive.

  ✅ **Reality:** AI budgeting simplifies finances clearly and privately. You remain fully in control of your financial data.

- ✖ **Myth:** AI savings are unreliable or risky.

  ✅ **Reality:** AI savings tools clearly set aside small, manageable amounts safely and securely—insured just like traditional bank accounts.

- ✖ **Myth:** Robo-advisors can lose your money easily.

  ✅ **Reality:** AI investing clearly emphasizes low-risk diversification, long-term growth, and consistent returns. While investing involves risk, robo-advisors actively manage and reduce that risk.

Quick Summary Table: AI in Personal Finance

Area of Personal Finance	AI Tools to Clearly Simplify Your Life
Budgeting	Mint, YNAB, EveryDollar (Clearly track expenses, control spending)
Saving	Digit, Qapital, Truebill (Clearly automate savings effortlessly)
Investing	Wealthfront, Betterment, Acorns (Clearly manage investments, build wealth easily)

📝 Why AI in Personal Finance Clearly Matters to You

Clearly leveraging AI financial tools practically transforms your money management:

- **Less Stress, More Control:**
  AI clearly simplifies budgeting, reducing financial anxiety and helping you feel confident about money.

- **Effortless Savings:**
  AI automatically grows your savings, building financial security easily and practically.

- **Smart Investing:**
  Clearly manage investments easily and confidently, clearly building wealth without complexity.

Simply put, AI makes financial management effortless, clear, and effective—helping you achieve financial freedom with ease.

⬤ Fitness & Wellness: AI Workout and Nutrition Helpers

Staying healthy can be challenging, especially with busy schedules, confusing fitness advice, and complicated diets. Fortunately, AI-powered fitness and wellness apps simplify this journey—clearly guiding your workouts, personalizing nutrition, and helping you achieve your health goals more easily and effectively than ever before.

In this chapter, we'll clearly explore how AI practically supports your fitness and nutrition goals. You'll discover exactly how AI simplifies staying active, eating well, and maintaining overall wellness—no matter how busy your life gets.

🏋️ AI-Powered Workouts: Personalized Fitness Made Easy

AI-powered fitness apps take the guesswork out of exercising by creating personalized workouts tailored exactly to your goals, fitness level, and schedule. Instead of generic routines, AI clearly designs custom programs, adapting workouts based on your progress, preferences, and even daily mood.

Exactly how AI enhances your workouts practically:

- **Personalized Training Plans:**
  AI clearly assesses your fitness level, sets realistic goals (weight loss, muscle gain, general fitness), and automatically builds workouts specifically designed for you.

- **Adaptive Workouts:**
  AI monitors your progress and clearly adjusts workouts in real-time, increasing or decreasing intensity based on your performance and feedback —ensuring optimal results without risk of injury.

- **Real-Time Coaching and Feedback:**
  AI-powered apps clearly guide you through exercises, correcting form, tracking reps, and motivating you like a personal trainer, but at a fraction of the cost.

AI Fitness App	Clear Benefits Clearly Explained
Fitbod	Creates personalized, adaptive workouts exactly for your goals
Nike Training Club	Provides custom fitness plans, real-time guidance
Freeletics	AI-driven workouts tailored to your fitness level and schedule

Clear, practical example:

Fitbod clearly notices you completed a leg workout yesterday. Today, it automatically creates an upper-body routine, clearly adjusting exercises based on your recent performance and recovery needs.

AI Nutrition Helpers: Effortless Healthy Eating

Eating healthy often feels confusing or restrictive—but AI nutrition apps simplify this clearly, creating personalized meal plans, tracking nutrients effortlessly, and helping you make healthier food choices daily.

Exactly how AI simplifies healthy eating practically:

- **Personalized Meal Plans:**
  AI analyzes your dietary preferences, health goals, and nutritional needs, then clearly creates easy-to-follow meal plans tailored exactly to you.

- **Automatic Nutrition Tracking:**
  AI apps like MyFitnessPal quickly recognize and log your meals simply by scanning barcodes or images, clearly tracking calories and nutrients without complicated effort.

- **Smart Recommendations:**
  AI suggests healthy alternatives clearly matched to your tastes, identifies nutrients you're missing, and helps you make smarter choices effortlessly.

AI Nutrition Tool	Clear Benefits to Your Daily Diet
MyFitnessPal	Automatic tracking, clearly personalized meal suggestions
Yazio	Tailored meal plans, easy nutrient tracking
Lose It!	Customized calorie goals, clear food logging

Clear, practical scenario:

MyFitnessPal clearly alerts you, "You're low on protein today," and suggests adding Greek yogurt or almonds clearly to balance your nutrients effortlessly.

🩺 AI for Health Monitoring and Wellness

AI also supports overall wellness by clearly monitoring your sleep, stress, and daily activity. Smartwatches and wearable devices (Fitbit, Apple Watch, Garmin) automatically track your health data, providing clear insights to help improve your lifestyle.

Exactly how AI wellness tracking practically helps:

- **Sleep Monitoring:**
  AI tracks sleep patterns (light, deep, REM sleep), clearly showing areas to improve your sleep quality for better energy and health.

- **Stress Management:**
  AI clearly analyzes your heart rate, breathing patterns, and daily habits to detect stress, clearly recommending relaxation techniques and activities to improve mental wellness.

- **Daily Activity Tracking:**
  AI tracks daily steps, calorie burn, and active minutes, clearly motivating you to remain active throughout your day effortlessly.

AI Wellness Device	Practical Benefits Clearly Explained
Fitbit, Garmin Watches	Clear sleep, stress, and activity tracking
Apple Watch	Daily wellness insights, heart health monitoring
Oura Ring	Advanced sleep and stress insights, clearly personalized

Clear, practical example:

Your smartwatch clearly detects increased stress levels midday, automatically suggesting a short guided breathing exercise to clearly relax and recharge.

▶ Common Misunderstandings Clarified

Clearly explaining common myths about AI fitness and wellness tools:

- ❌ **Myth:** AI workouts and diets are too generic or impersonal.
  ✅ **Reality:** AI creates clearly personalized, adaptive plans exactly matched to your unique needs, goals, and preferences.

- ❌ **Myth:** AI wellness tracking invades privacy or feels intrusive.
  ✅ **Reality:** Wellness devices clearly offer strong privacy controls, giving you complete control over your data. They only use information clearly to help you personally—not to share publicly.

- ❌ **Myth:** AI nutrition apps only track calories or restrict food choices.
  ✅ **Reality:** AI clearly offers balanced, practical meal plans based on nutritional goals—not restrictive dieting—making healthy eating easier and enjoyable.

📋 Quick Summary Table: AI in Fitness & Wellness

Area of Fitness & Wellness	AI Tools Clearly Improving Your Life
Workouts & Fitness	Fitbod, Nike Training Club, Freeletics (Clearly personalized workouts)
Nutrition & Diet	MyFitnessPal, Yazio, Lose It! (Clearly personalized nutrition plans)
Health & Wellness	Fitbit, Garmin, Apple Watch, Oura Ring (Clearly monitoring sleep, stress, and activity)

📝 Why AI Clearly Matters for Your Fitness and Wellness

Clearly using AI-powered fitness and wellness tools practically transforms your health journey:

- **Personalized Guidance:**
  AI clearly customizes workouts and meals exactly for your needs, preferences, and goals—maximizing your results without confusion.

- **Motivation and Accountability:**
  AI clearly tracks progress, offers real-time feedback, and motivates you consistently, keeping you focused and inspired.

- **Better Overall Health:**
  AI clearly monitors your sleep, stress, diet, and activity, clearly guiding you towards healthier, happier living without extra effort.

Simply put, AI makes achieving your fitness and wellness goals clearer, simpler, and easier than ever.

Mental Health Apps: Can AI Really Help You Feel Better?

Mental health is just as important as physical health—but finding practical, affordable, and accessible emotional support can be challenging. AI-powered mental health apps are now helping millions manage stress, anxiety, depression, and emotional well-being clearly and easily, providing instant support exactly when you need it most.

In this chapter, we'll clearly examine how AI mental health apps practically support your emotional wellness, exactly how effective they truly are, and how you can best use these tools in your everyday life to feel better, reduce stress, and maintain mental balance.

How AI Mental Health Apps Really Work

AI-powered mental health apps use techniques like Cognitive Behavioral Therapy (CBT), mindfulness, emotional tracking, and personalized support clearly adapted to your unique emotional needs. These apps act as instant digital companions—providing practical guidance, emotional support, and stress-relief anytime you need it, privately and affordably.

Here's exactly how AI mental health apps practically help:

- **Instant Emotional Support:**
  Apps clearly provide immediate support during moments of stress or anxiety, guiding you through

calming exercises, breathing techniques, or positive thinking clearly and effectively.

- **Personalized Guidance:**
  AI clearly learns your emotional patterns and triggers, offering personalized suggestions for managing stress, reducing anxiety, or boosting your mood based on your unique emotional profile.

- **Daily Mood and Progress Tracking:**
  AI tracks your daily emotional health clearly, providing insights, identifying patterns, and helping you clearly understand emotional triggers or behaviors.

A clear practical example:

Feeling anxious at work? An AI mental health app clearly notices increased stress levels and instantly suggests a quick, guided breathing exercise to calm you down— helping you quickly regain emotional balance.

▦ Popular AI Mental Health Apps Clearly Explained

Here are clearly explained examples of popular, effective AI mental health apps available today:

AI Mental Health App	Clearly Practical Benefits for Your Well-Being
Woebot	AI chatbot offering CBT techniques, stress reduction, and instant emotional support.
Wysa	Clearly personalized emotional support, anxiety management, and mindfulness exercises.
Youper	Tracks emotions clearly, identifies patterns, and provides personalized therapy exercises.
Headspace, Calm	AI-powered mindfulness, meditation, and sleep improvement clearly guided and personalized.

Clear practical scenario:

Woebot clearly checks in daily, asking "How are you feeling today?" Based on your response, it clearly guides you through personalized exercises, gently helping you manage stress or negative emotions.

🧠 Can AI Mental Health Apps Actually Help? (Clear Evidence)

Research shows AI mental health apps genuinely help reduce stress, anxiety, and mild-to-moderate depression for many users. Clearly summarized evidence:

- **Reducing Anxiety:**
  Studies show apps like Woebot and Wysa significantly reduce anxiety symptoms clearly by providing practical emotional support and teaching effective coping strategies.

- **Improving Emotional Well-being:**
  Users consistently report improved mood, clearer thinking, reduced stress, and greater emotional control after regularly using AI mental health apps.

- **Accessibility and Convenience:**
  Clearly, the greatest benefit is convenience—AI apps are affordable, instantly available, and private, removing barriers like cost, stigma, or limited availability of human therapists.

AI Mental Health App	Proven Effectiveness Clearly Summarized
Woebot	Clearly reduces anxiety and depression symptoms, proven in multiple scientific studies.
Wysa	Proven effective at managing anxiety, sleep issues, and emotional distress.
Headspace, Calm	Strongly supported by research clearly showing improved mental health, reduced stress.

Simply put, yes — AI mental health apps genuinely help users practically and clearly manage emotional health, especially as an accessible, immediate support option.

▶ Limitations Clearly Explained (What AI Can't Do)

Clearly recognizing limitations of AI mental health apps helps set realistic expectations:

- **Not a Complete Substitute for Therapy:**
  While effective for mild-to-moderate emotional challenges, AI apps clearly aren't replacements for professional therapists, especially for severe mental health conditions.

- **Limited Emotional Understanding:**
  AI can clearly offer practical suggestions and exercises, but it doesn't genuinely feel empathy or fully understand complex emotions in the human sense.

- **Best as Complementary Tools:**
  AI mental health apps work best clearly as supplemental tools alongside professional support, human connections, and self-care strategies.

Clear practical limitations summarized:

AI Mental Health Apps Clearly Can Do	Clearly Cannot Do (Yet)
✓ Provide instant emotional support	✗ Completely replace human therapists
✓ Clearly teach coping skills, mindfulness	✗ Understand complex emotional experiences deeply
✓ Improve emotional well-being for many	✗ Effectively manage severe mental health disorders

📌 How to Clearly Benefit Most from AI Mental Health Apps

Clearly following these practical tips helps you gain maximum benefits from AI mental health apps:

- ✅ **Use Daily for Best Results:**
  Regular daily interactions clearly strengthen emotional coping skills, build resilience, and consistently improve emotional well-being.

- ✅ **Be Open and Honest:**
  Clearly share genuine feelings and challenges—AI apps provide more practical, effective guidance when they understand your true emotional state.

- ✅ **Combine with Professional Help:**
  Clearly use AI apps alongside professional therapy if needed, amplifying benefits and providing continuous, accessible emotional support.

📝 Why AI Mental Health Apps Clearly Matter for You

Clearly incorporating AI mental health apps into your daily life practically enhances emotional health and overall well-being:

- **Instant, Accessible Support:**
  Clearly provides emotional help exactly when you need it most—day or night.

- **Affordable and Private:**
  Clearly removes financial and social barriers to emotional support.

- **Effective Stress and Anxiety Reduction:**
  Clearly proven to practically improve emotional health, reduce anxiety, and boost overall mood and mental clarity.

Simply put, AI mental health apps offer a practical, clear, and genuinely effective way to maintain emotional health, reduce daily stress, and improve your quality of life effortlessly.

⬤ Using AI to Learn Anything Faster (Duolingo, Khan, etc.)

Learning new things—whether it's a language, a musical instrument, or academic subjects—can feel overwhelming, time-consuming, or frustratingly slow. Thankfully, Artificial Intelligence (AI) makes learning clearly faster, easier, and more effective than ever, personalizing your education exactly to your strengths, interests, and pace.

In this chapter, we'll clearly explore exactly how AI-powered learning apps practically accelerate your progress, provide personalized guidance, and make learning enjoyable and efficient—so you can learn anything faster, better, and without stress.

📚 How AI Makes Learning Easier and Faster (Clearly Explained)

AI transforms learning by personalizing education specifically for your needs, skills, and learning style. Instead of generic lessons, AI analyzes your progress clearly and continuously, instantly adapting to help you master new concepts faster.

Here's exactly how AI practically enhances your learning:

- **Personalized Learning Paths:**
  AI instantly identifies your strengths and weaknesses, clearly customizing lessons to match your learning level, ensuring you learn quickly without frustration.

- **Adaptive Difficulty Levels:**
  AI automatically adjusts lessons clearly and
  instantly, ensuring you remain challenged but never
  overwhelmed, creating a smooth learning
  experience that speeds up progress.

- **Instant Feedback and Correction:**
  AI clearly identifies your mistakes immediately,
  providing instant corrections and explanations, so
  you quickly understand errors and avoid repeating
  them.

Clear practical example:

Learning Spanish on Duolingo, you struggle clearly with
past tense verbs. AI automatically provides extra practice
specifically on these verbs, clearly helping you master
them quickly without confusion.

🌍 Learning Languages Clearly and Quickly (Duolingo, Babbel)

Language learning is one of the clearest and most
practical areas where AI has revolutionized education.
Apps like Duolingo and Babbel use AI to help millions
master new languages clearly and efficiently.

**Exactly how AI language apps clearly speed your
progress:**

- **Real-time Practice:**
  AI clearly recognizes words and grammar you
  struggle with, instantly reinforcing practice in those
  areas to quickly build confidence and fluency.

- **Personalized Exercises:**
  AI customizes lessons exactly to your current level,

clearly adjusting difficulty based on real-time performance, ensuring fast and steady progress.

- **Motivational Reminders:**
  AI clearly keeps you engaged and motivated with daily reminders, streaks, rewards, and progress tracking, making consistent practice easy and enjoyable.

AI Language Learning App	Clearly Explained Practical Benefits
Duolingo	Clearly personalized lessons, adaptive practice, motivating streaks
Babbel	Practical conversations, clear personalized courses, instant feedback
Rosetta Stone	Clearly customized language paths, adaptive practice

Clear practical scenario:

You consistently make mistakes clearly using French prepositions. Duolingo's AI immediately recognizes this, offering personalized exercises clearly focused exactly on prepositions until you master them easily.

🎓 AI in Education: Faster Learning with Khan Academy

AI isn't just for language learning—it clearly transforms academic subjects too. Khan Academy uses AI clearly to personalize learning in math, science, and other subjects, helping students quickly master new concepts at their own pace.

Exactly how Khan Academy's AI clearly speeds up learning:

- **Personalized Skill Recommendations:**
  AI clearly identifies your skill level instantly, recommending exactly which topics or exercises you need to practice most.

- **Instant, Detailed Feedback:**
  AI immediately shows you clearly how to correct mistakes, providing practical explanations to help you quickly learn from errors.

- **Adaptive Progression:**
  AI continuously monitors your progress clearly, automatically adjusting lesson difficulty and topics to keep you moving forward confidently.

AI Educational App	Clearly Explained Practical Benefits
Khan Academy	Clearly personalized learning, instant feedback, adaptive exercises
Coursera, edX	Clearly personalized course recommendations, adaptive content
Quizlet	Clearly adaptive flashcards, personalized practice, quick mastery

Clear practical scenario:

Khan Academy clearly identifies you're struggling with algebraic equations. AI automatically provides additional, clearly explained practice problems exactly matched to your needs, helping you quickly master the topic confidently.

🎵 AI for Creative Learning (Music, Art, Coding)

AI clearly simplifies learning new creative skills—music instruments, drawing, or coding—by providing personalized lessons, real-time guidance, and adaptive practice tailored exactly to your progress and abilities.

Exactly how AI clearly helps with creative learning:

- **Real-time Feedback:**
  AI clearly provides immediate guidance while playing an instrument or coding, instantly correcting mistakes and clearly showing you how to improve.

- **Adaptive Practice Sessions:**
  AI continuously monitors your skills clearly, adjusting practice sessions exactly to your ability level to accelerate learning quickly.

- **Step-by-step Skill Building:**
  AI breaks complex skills clearly into manageable lessons, ensuring steady and confident progress.

AI Creative Learning Apps	Clearly Explained Practical Benefits
Yousician (Music)	Clearly personalized lessons, instant feedback, adaptive music practice
Simply Piano	AI-guided piano lessons clearly matched exactly to your skill level
Grasshopper (Coding)	Clearly adaptive coding lessons, personalized practice

Clear practical scenario:

Learning guitar on Yousician, AI clearly identifies you're struggling with chord transitions. It immediately provides clearly targeted exercises specifically improving your chord-changing speed and accuracy.

▶ Common Misunderstandings Clearly Explained

Clearly addressing myths about AI learning:

- ✖ **Myth:** AI learning tools provide generic, impersonal lessons.
  ☑ **Reality:** AI clearly personalizes lessons exactly for you, continuously adapting and responding directly to your needs.

- ✖ **Myth:** AI learning completely replaces teachers or human instruction.
  ☑ **Reality:** AI clearly complements human teaching, providing extra personalized practice and immediate feedback clearly beneficial to any learning process.

- ✖ **Myth:** AI learning only works for certain topics or subjects.
  ☑ **Reality:** AI practically enhances learning across almost any skill or subject, clearly personalizing your education and speeding up your progress.

📋 Quick Summary Table: AI in Learning Clearly Summarized

Learning Area	Clearly Explained AI Tools Making You Learn Faster
Languages	Duolingo, Babbel, Rosetta Stone (Clearly personalized, adaptive learning)
Academic Subjects	Khan Academy, Coursera, Quizlet (Clearly personalized, adaptive practice)
Creative Skills	Yousician, Simply Piano, Grasshopper (Clearly personalized, real-time feedback)

Why AI Clearly Matters for Faster Learning

Clearly using AI-powered learning apps practically transforms your educational journey:

- **Personalized Learning:**
  AI clearly customizes education exactly for your strengths and weaknesses, speeding up mastery.

- **Immediate, Clear Feedback:**
  AI provides instant corrections clearly helping you quickly learn from mistakes.

- **Efficient Progress:**
  AI clearly adapts lessons continuously, ensuring steady progress without frustration or wasted time.

Simply put, AI clearly makes learning faster, easier, and more enjoyable than ever, practically helping you master any new skill confidently and efficiently.

⬤ AI for Parents and Families: Help, Play & Learning Tools

Parenting can be both incredibly rewarding and deeply challenging—especially when balancing work, family schedules, children's learning, and playtime. Thankfully, Artificial Intelligence (AI) now clearly provides practical, helpful tools for parents and families, making daily life easier, more organized, and enriching for kids of all ages.

In this chapter, we'll clearly explore exactly how AI supports family life—simplifying parenting tasks, helping children learn and grow, and making playtime educational and enjoyable. You'll discover practical AI tools designed specifically to enhance family routines, provide peace of mind, and ensure your children thrive.

👪 AI Tools Clearly Simplifying Family Life

Modern families juggle busy schedules, daily responsibilities, and children's needs. AI clearly simplifies these challenges—automatically managing routines, organizing family calendars, and reducing stress so parents can focus on meaningful interactions.

Exactly how AI practically supports family management:

- **Smart Family Calendars:**
  AI clearly coordinates schedules—school events, sports practices, doctor's appointments—and automatically sends reminders, keeping everyone organized effortlessly.

- **Automated Task Management:**
  AI clearly assigns chores, tracks completion, and motivates children with rewards, clearly simplifying daily responsibilities and encouraging independence.

- **Real-Time Family Safety and Location:**
  AI-powered location apps clearly provide instant updates about children's whereabouts, giving parents peace of mind clearly and immediately.

Clear practical example:

AI-powered apps like **Life360** clearly notify you when your child arrives safely at school or home, providing immediate reassurance without constant calls or texts.

AI Family Management Tool	Clearly Explained Practical Benefits
Cozi Family Organizer	Clearly manages calendars, tasks, family reminders
Life360	Instant family location updates clearly for safety
Google Family Link	Clearly manages children's device use, screen time

👧 AI Tools Clearly Supporting Children's Learning and Growth

AI provides clear, personalized educational support for children of all ages, enhancing learning, building essential skills, and adapting exactly to each child's unique developmental needs.

Exactly how AI clearly helps children's learning:

- **Personalized Learning Apps:**
  AI-powered apps like Khan Academy Kids clearly adapt content exactly to your child's developmental stage, interests, and learning pace, ensuring effective and engaging learning.

- **Reading and Literacy Support:**
  AI clearly assists children in reading practice, pronunciation, and vocabulary building—providing immediate feedback to accelerate learning confidently.

- **Math and STEM Education:**
  AI apps clearly make math and science fun and approachable, providing personalized exercises that match exactly your child's learning level, helping them build confidence and master skills.

Clear practical scenario:

Your child struggles clearly with reading comprehension. AI-powered apps like **Reading Eggs** identify this quickly, providing personalized activities exactly targeting comprehension skills, improving reading confidence practically and effectively.

AI Children's Learning Apps	Clearly Explained Practical Benefits
Khan Academy Kids	Personalized learning exactly matched to your child's needs
Reading Eggs	Clearly improves reading skills with personalized exercises
Prodigy Math Game	Clearly makes math fun, personalized practice and progress tracking

🎲 AI in Family Play and Entertainment

Playtime clearly matters for family bonding and children's development. AI-powered games and entertainment apps make family play engaging, educational, and enjoyable—clearly fostering creativity, critical thinking, and meaningful interactions.

Exactly how AI clearly enriches family playtime:

- **Interactive Storytelling:**
  AI-powered interactive books and stories clearly adapt narratives based exactly on your child's choices, interests, and reactions, promoting creativity and curiosity.

- **Educational Games:**
  AI clearly personalizes game difficulty and content exactly to children's skill levels, ensuring games remain both challenging and achievable, encouraging continuous learning and engagement.

- **Family-Friendly AI Voice Assistants:**
  Smart speakers (Alexa, Google Home) clearly provide family-friendly games, trivia, and interactive activities clearly enjoyable for all ages.

Clear practical example:

Playing **Osmo** interactive games, your child clearly solves puzzles, practices spelling, or learns basic coding—all tailored exactly to their current skills and interests, keeping playtime educational and engaging.

AI Family Play Tools	Clearly Explained Practical Benefits
Osmo	Clearly personalized interactive games, educational play
Amazon Alexa Kids	Family-friendly interactive voice games, clearly enjoyable
Toca Boca Apps	Clearly engaging play experiences exactly tailored to kids

🛡 AI Clearly Providing Family Safety and Peace of Mind

Keeping your family safe clearly matters above all else. AI enhances safety practically—clearly monitoring digital activities, filtering inappropriate content, and ensuring children's online safety without constant parental worry.

Exactly how AI clearly protects family safety:

- **Smart Parental Controls:**
  AI clearly monitors screen time, manages device usage, and automatically filters inappropriate content clearly and immediately, ensuring your child's safe online experience.

- **Instant Safety Alerts:**
  AI clearly detects potential issues—like inappropriate messages, bullying, or suspicious activities—and immediately alerts parents practically, allowing quick intervention and peace of mind.

AI Family Safety Tool	Clearly Explained Practical Benefits
Bark	Clearly monitors children's digital activity, instant alerts
Qustodio	Clearly manages screen time, content filtering practically
Net Nanny	Clearly ensures safe online browsing, instant parental notifications

Clear practical example:

Bark AI clearly detects signs of cyberbullying in your child's text messages, instantly notifying you practically and privately—enabling you to support your child clearly and quickly.

▶ **Common Misunderstandings Clearly Explained**

Clearly clarifying myths about AI parenting tools:

- ✖ **Myth:** AI parenting tools completely replace parental involvement.
✅ **Reality:** AI clearly supports parenting practically, providing assistance and peace of mind but not replacing meaningful parent-child interactions.

- ✖ **Myth:** AI learning and playtime are impersonal or ineffective.
✅ **Reality:** AI clearly personalizes learning and play exactly to your child's needs, practically enhancing educational and developmental outcomes.

- ❌ **Myth:** AI family tools invade privacy or limit children's freedom.

  ✅ **Reality:** AI clearly provides safety and support practically, with strong parental controls ensuring clear privacy and safe boundaries without excessive intrusion.

📋 Quick Summary Table: AI in Parenting and Family Life Clearly Summarized

Family Life Area	Clearly Explained AI Tools Practically Helping You
Family Organization	Cozi, Life360, Google Family Link (Clearly organizes family life)
Children's Learning	Khan Academy Kids, Reading Eggs, Prodigy (Clearly personalized learning)
Play and Entertainment	Osmo, Alexa Kids, Toca Boca (Clearly educational, engaging play)
Family Safety & Security	Bark, Qustodio, Net Nanny (Clearly protecting family safety practically)

📝 Why AI Clearly Matters for Parents and Families

Clearly integrating AI into family life practically enhances parenting, children's learning, playtime, and overall family harmony:

- **Easier Family Management:**
  AI clearly organizes busy schedules, simplifies routines, and reduces daily stress.

- **Personalized Children's Learning:**
  AI clearly adapts education exactly to your child's needs, practically boosting learning outcomes.

- **Enhanced Family Safety:**
  AI clearly monitors and protects children practically, ensuring safety without constant worry.

Simply put, AI clearly makes parenting easier, family life more enjoyable, and children's development more successful.

SECTION 3

AI AT WORK AND IN BUSINESS

(Boosting productivity, saving time, and simplifying processes)

● AI for Email, Documents, Presentations (Google, Microsoft, Notion)

Creating emails, documents, and presentations can quickly consume hours of your day. Whether it's drafting professional emails, formatting lengthy documents, or designing compelling slides, these tasks often feel repetitive and time-consuming. Thankfully, Artificial Intelligence (AI) clearly simplifies these processes, practically enhancing productivity and efficiency across tools like Google Workspace, Microsoft 365, and Notion.

In this chapter, we'll clearly explore exactly how AI helps you quickly create professional emails, produce polished documents, and design effective presentations—making everyday office tasks faster, simpler, and stress-free.

▄ AI for Email: Clear, Quick, Professional

Email is essential but can easily become overwhelming. AI-powered email tools clearly help you compose, manage, and respond to emails quickly, professionally, and effortlessly.

Exactly how AI practically helps with email:

- **Smart Compose (Google Gmail, Outlook):** AI clearly suggests complete sentences instantly while typing emails, speeding up drafting significantly and ensuring professional, clear language.

- **Automatic Email Summarization:** AI quickly summarizes lengthy email threads into clear, concise points, saving you from lengthy reading and improving productivity practically.

- **Intelligent Email Sorting:**
  AI automatically categorizes emails (priority, spam, updates) clearly and accurately, ensuring you quickly see important messages and reduce clutter.

AI Email Tool	Clearly Explained Practical Benefits
Gmail Smart Compose	Instantly suggests professional phrases, clearly saves writing time
Microsoft Outlook AI	Clearly summarizes emails, prioritizes important messages automatically
Grammarly for Email	Clearly enhances grammar and readability instantly

Clear practical scenario:

Writing a follow-up email? Gmail's Smart Compose clearly suggests sentences like "Just following up on my previous email," instantly completing your message professionally and effortlessly.

AI for Documents: Faster Writing and Editing

Creating and editing professional documents is essential —but also highly time-consuming. AI-powered document tools practically enhance your efficiency, clarity, and productivity clearly and easily.

Exactly how AI clearly simplifies document tasks:

- **Automatic Grammar and Style Improvements:**
  AI tools like Grammarly and Microsoft Editor instantly correct spelling, grammar, and clarity clearly, making your documents polished and professional with minimal effort.

- **Intelligent Formatting and Templates:**
  AI clearly suggests layouts, formatting, and templates based exactly on document types (reports, resumes, letters), dramatically speeding up your workflow practically.

- **Content Generation and Summarization:**
  AI instantly generates content outlines, summarizes lengthy documents, and clearly suggests improvements, helping you produce high-quality documents rapidly.

AI Document Tool	Clearly Explained Practical Benefits
Google Docs AI	Clearly assists writing, formatting, and instantly creates outlines
Microsoft Word AI	Clearly corrects grammar/style, suggests formatting practically
Notion AI	Instantly generates content outlines, clearly structures documents efficiently

Clear practical example:

Creating a project report in Google Docs? AI clearly suggests professional formatting, instantly generates clear section outlines, and helps draft summaries practically, significantly reducing your workload.

AI for Presentations: Professional, Engaging, Quick

Crafting engaging presentations clearly takes time and creativity. AI-powered presentation tools practically simplify design, content creation, and slide organization, helping you quickly build compelling, professional presentations.

Exactly how AI clearly improves presentations practically:

- **Automatic Slide Creation and Formatting:**
  AI instantly generates slide layouts, chooses clear, professional themes, and automatically formats slides exactly to your content type, dramatically simplifying the process.

- **Instant Content Suggestions:**
  AI clearly suggests presentation content, bullet points, and images based on your topic, practically helping you create informative slides rapidly.

- **Speaker Notes and Speech Support:**
  AI clearly creates concise speaker notes, suggests key points, and even provides real-time speech coaching, enhancing your delivery practically.

AI Presentation Tool	Clearly Explained Practical Benefits
Google Slides AI	Instantly generates professional layouts, clearly simplifies slide creation
Microsoft PowerPoint AI	Clearly provides smart design ideas, real-time presentation coaching
Beautiful.ai	Automatically creates visually engaging slides clearly and professionally

Clear practical scenario:

You quickly need slides for tomorrow's meeting. PowerPoint AI clearly suggests visually appealing layouts and relevant content based on your outline, practically completing your presentation in minutes, not hours.

⚡ Comparing AI Capabilities: Google vs. Microsoft vs. Notion

Each platform clearly offers distinct AI strengths tailored exactly to your professional needs:

Platform Feature	Google Workspace AI	Microsoft 365 AI	Notion AI
Email Productivity	Excellent Smart Compose, priority inbox clearly simplifies emails	Powerful summarization, professional email drafting practically	Not applicable
Document Creation	Quick outlines, automatic grammar improvements clearly simplify writing	Advanced editing, formatting, clear grammar/style corrections	Fast content generation, clear document structuring instantly
Presentations	Smart slide layouts, instant formatting clearly speeds up slides	Smart design ideas, clear speaker coaching practically	Not directly applicable

- **Google Workspace:** Clearly excels in email productivity, quick document creation, and straightforward presentations.

- **Microsoft 365:** Clearly powerful for detailed editing, formatting, and professional presentations.

- **Notion AI:** Clearly best for quick content generation, structured documents, and creative workflows.

▶ Common Misunderstandings Clearly Explained

Clearly clarifying myths about AI productivity tools:

- ❌ **Myth:** AI completely replaces human input in emails and documents.

  ✅ **Reality:** AI clearly enhances human writing practically, significantly speeding up tasks while maintaining your personal tone and style.

- ❌ **Myth:** AI-generated presentations lack originality or creativity.

  ✅ **Reality:** AI clearly supports creativity practically, providing professional layouts and content suggestions exactly tailored to your message.

- ❌ **Myth:** AI writing and formatting always produce robotic, unnatural results.

  ✅ **Reality:** AI practically generates highly professional, natural-sounding content clearly enhancing your original ideas.

📋 **Quick Summary Table: AI Productivity in Emails, Documents, Presentations**

Productivity Task	Clearly Explained Best AI Tools
Emails & Communication	Gmail Smart Compose, Outlook AI, Grammarly
Document Writing	Google Docs AI, Microsoft Word AI, Notion AI
Presentations & Slides	Google Slides AI, PowerPoint AI, Beautiful.ai

📝 **Why AI Clearly Matters for Professional Productivity**

Clearly integrating AI practically enhances productivity, efficiency, and quality across emails, documents, and presentations:

- **Significantly Reduced Time and Effort:**
  AI clearly simplifies writing, formatting, and designing practically, completing tasks in a fraction of the usual time.

- **Improved Professional Quality:**
  AI instantly enhances grammar, clarity, and design practically, ensuring consistently professional outputs clearly and effortlessly.

- **Enhanced Creativity and Confidence:**
  AI clearly generates content ideas and professional layouts practically, boosting creativity and confidence in all your professional communications.

Simply put, AI productivity tools clearly help you work faster, smarter, and more professionally—dramatically simplifying everyday office tasks.

● Automate Repetitive Tasks: Calendars, CRM, Data Entry

At work, repetitive tasks—like scheduling meetings, managing customer information, or manually entering data—often drain your energy, waste valuable hours, and distract you from meaningful tasks. Thankfully, Artificial Intelligence (AI) clearly automates these repetitive processes, practically saving you significant time, reducing mistakes, and freeing your focus for higher-value work.

In this chapter, we'll clearly explore exactly how AI practically simplifies and automates calendars, Customer Relationship Management (CRM), and data entry tasks—dramatically boosting your productivity and efficiency at work.

17 AI for Calendars: Automating Scheduling Effortlessly

Scheduling meetings or coordinating calendars often consumes unnecessary time. AI-powered calendar tools practically automate this process, instantly arranging meetings clearly and effortlessly.

Exactly how AI clearly automates your calendar:

- **Smart Meeting Scheduling:**
  AI clearly checks availability, suggests optimal meeting times automatically, and handles invitations—eliminating back-and-forth emails practically.

- **Intelligent Reminders and Notifications:**
  AI clearly learns your habits, sending automatic reminders exactly when you need them, ensuring you never miss appointments or deadlines.

- **Automatic Time Management:**
  AI practically analyzes your schedule, identifies optimal productivity windows, and suggests time blocks for focused work clearly and automatically.

AI Calendar Tool	Clearly Explained Practical Benefits
Calendly	Instantly automates meeting scheduling clearly
Google Calendar AI	Clearly suggests best meeting times, automatic reminders
Microsoft Outlook Scheduler	Clearly handles meeting requests, scheduling practically

Clear practical scenario:

Need a quick team meeting? Calendly AI clearly identifies everyone's availability, instantly suggests a convenient time, and automatically sends invitations—saving significant scheduling time practically.

🤝 AI in CRM: Automating Customer Relationship Management

Customer Relationship Management (CRM) involves repetitive tasks like data entry, tracking leads, or sending follow-ups. AI-powered CRM tools clearly automate these tasks practically, making customer management efficient, accurate, and stress-free.

Exactly how AI practically simplifies CRM tasks:

- **Automatic Lead Management:**
  AI instantly sorts leads based on priority, tracks interactions clearly, and sends personalized follow-up emails automatically, ensuring no potential customers slip through the cracks practically.

- **Smart Customer Insights:**
  AI clearly analyzes customer data, predicts customer needs, and suggests proactive actions—helping you build stronger relationships practically and clearly.

- **Automated Data Updates:**
  AI automatically updates customer records practically in real-time, ensuring data accuracy clearly without manual input, eliminating mistakes.

AI CRM Tool	Clearly Explained Practical Benefits
Salesforce Einstein	Clearly automates lead management, predictive customer insights
HubSpot CRM AI	Instantly updates customer data clearly, automates email follow-ups
Zoho CRM AI	Clearly predicts customer behavior, automates task management practically

Clear practical example:

HubSpot CRM AI clearly detects when a prospect opens your email. It instantly sends a personalized follow-up, practically automating your sales process and boosting customer engagement clearly.

📑 AI for Data Entry: Accurate, Automated, Effortless

Data entry tasks are often tedious, error-prone, and time-consuming. AI-powered tools clearly automate data entry practically, ensuring accuracy and saving substantial work hours clearly and effortlessly.

Exactly how AI practically automates data entry tasks:

- **Intelligent Data Extraction:**
  AI automatically reads invoices, receipts, or emails practically, instantly extracting accurate data clearly into your databases without manual entry.

- **Error Reduction and Validation:**
  AI clearly identifies data entry errors immediately, automatically correcting inaccuracies practically, dramatically improving data reliability.

- **Automated Document Processing:**
  AI quickly and clearly converts paper documents or scanned images into digital formats, practically reducing manual input and speeding up workflows significantly.

AI Data Entry Tool	Clearly Explained Practical Benefits
Zapier, Make (Integromat)	Clearly connects apps, automates data entry instantly
Rossum AI	Clearly automates document data extraction practically
UiPath, Automation Anywhere	Clearly automates repetitive tasks instantly and accurately

Clear practical scenario:

You receive multiple invoices daily. Rossum AI clearly reads each invoice, instantly extracting necessary details (amount, date, vendor) clearly into your accounting software automatically—saving countless hours of manual input practically.

⚡ AI Automation Clearly Compared: Calendars, CRM, Data Entry

Here's a clear comparison of how AI automation practically improves productivity across these repetitive tasks:

Task Category	Clearly Explained Automation Benefits	Popular AI Tools
Calendar Management	Automatic scheduling, reminders, clearly simplified meetings	Calendly, Google Calendar AI, Outlook Scheduler
CRM & Customer Management	Instantly manages leads, predicts customer needs clearly	Salesforce Einstein, HubSpot CRM AI, Zoho CRM AI
Data Entry & Processing	Quickly extracts data, reduces errors, clearly automates input	Zapier, Rossum AI, UiPath

▶ Common Misunderstandings Clearly Explained

Clearly clarifying myths about AI task automation:

- ❌ **Myth:** AI automation replaces human jobs entirely.

  ✅ **Reality:** AI clearly automates repetitive tasks practically, freeing humans for higher-value work requiring creativity and judgment.

- ✖ **Myth:** Automated CRM tools lack personal touch.

  ☑ **Reality:** AI practically provides highly personalized interactions clearly based on customer data, enhancing customer relationships effectively.

- ✖ **Myth:** AI automated data entry is inaccurate or unreliable.

  ☑ **Reality:** AI clearly reduces data entry errors practically, dramatically improving accuracy and reliability compared to manual entry.

📋 **Quick Summary Table: AI Automation Clearly Summarized**

Automation Area	Clearly Explained Practical AI Benefits	Recommended AI Tools
Calendars & Scheduling	Instantly automates meetings clearly	Calendly, Google Calendar AI
CRM & Customer Management	Clearly manages leads, automates follow-ups practically	Salesforce Einstein, HubSpot AI
Data Entry & Document Handling	Quickly extracts data, clearly reduces errors practically	Zapier, Rossum AI, UiPath

Why AI Automation Clearly Matters for Your Productivity

Clearly integrating AI automation practically transforms your workflow, reduces stress, and significantly boosts your efficiency and accuracy:

- **Dramatic Time Savings:**
  AI clearly automates repetitive tasks practically, saving countless hours weekly and boosting productivity instantly.

- **Enhanced Accuracy and Reliability:**
  AI practically eliminates manual errors clearly, ensuring consistent, accurate results across calendars, CRM, and data entry.

- **Greater Focus on High-Value Work:**
  AI clearly frees your time practically, allowing you to concentrate clearly on strategic, creative tasks that truly matter.

Simply put, AI automation clearly makes your professional life easier, more productive, and less stressful —practically improving your daily work experience.

● AI for Freelancers: Research, Marketing, Client Work

Freelancing offers incredible freedom, but it also comes with unique challenges—juggling multiple clients, marketing your services, researching projects, and managing deadlines. Artificial Intelligence (AI) clearly simplifies and streamlines freelance tasks, practically helping you work faster, smarter, and more efficiently.

In this chapter, we'll clearly explore exactly how AI supports freelancers—accelerating research, simplifying marketing, and effortlessly managing client work. You'll discover practical tools that clearly help you become more productive, organized, and successful in your freelance career.

🔍 AI for Freelance Research: Faster, Easier, Accurate

Researching new topics or client projects often consumes valuable hours. AI-powered research tools practically speed up the research process, instantly providing clear, accurate information exactly when you need it.

Exactly how AI clearly simplifies freelance research:

- **Instant Information Summaries:**
  AI quickly summarizes lengthy articles, reports, or research papers clearly, providing concise points and practically saving you significant reading time.

- **Efficient Fact-Checking:**
  AI instantly verifies facts and data clearly, ensuring accuracy and reliability in your freelance work practically.

- **Idea Generation and Content Outlines:**
  AI clearly helps brainstorm content ideas, generates structured outlines practically, and streamlines your research workflow significantly.

AI Research Tool	Clearly Explained Practical Benefits
ChatGPT, Perplexity AI	Clearly summarizes complex information instantly
Consensus, SciSpace	Quickly verifies facts, finds accurate research clearly
Notion AI, Jasper AI	Instantly generates content ideas and outlines clearly

Clear practical scenario:

You're writing an article on sustainability. AI clearly summarizes recent studies, instantly generates a structured outline, and practically provides accurate facts—saving hours of manual research clearly.

📢 AI for Freelance Marketing: Attract Clients Effortlessly

Marketing your freelance services clearly requires consistent content creation, client outreach, and engaging messaging. AI-powered marketing tools practically automate and simplify these tasks, clearly helping you attract and retain clients effectively.

Exactly how AI clearly enhances freelance marketing:

- **Instant Content Creation:**
  AI practically generates compelling blog posts, social media updates, and emails instantly—clearly showcasing your services without endless content writing.

125

- **Automated Social Media Management:**
  AI clearly schedules posts, analyzes performance, and practically optimizes your social media presence effortlessly, attracting more clients clearly.

- **Personalized Client Outreach:**
  AI clearly generates professional emails and messages practically tailored exactly to potential clients, simplifying outreach and increasing response rates.

AI Marketing Tool	Clearly Explained Practical Benefits
ChatGPT, Jasper AI	Instantly creates engaging marketing content clearly
Buffer, Later AI	Clearly automates social media management practically
Grammarly, Mailchimp AI	Practically enhances emails, personalized client outreach

Clear practical example:

Need engaging LinkedIn posts? AI clearly generates professional posts instantly, practically enhancing your online presence and attracting new freelance clients effortlessly.

AI for Client Work Management: Clear, Organized, Efficient

Managing multiple freelance clients clearly involves scheduling tasks, tracking progress, and organizing projects. AI-powered management tools practically streamline client work, clearly boosting your efficiency and ensuring consistent professionalism.

Exactly how AI clearly helps manage freelance client work:

- **Automatic Task Management and Reminders:** AI clearly organizes deadlines, automatically tracks tasks, and practically sends timely reminders, ensuring client projects remain on schedule clearly.

- **Client Communication and Follow-ups:** AI practically drafts professional client messages, sends automatic follow-ups clearly, and ensures consistent, clear communication effortlessly.

- **Efficient Project Organization:** AI clearly creates project outlines, organizes documents practically, and streamlines workflows —reducing stress and enhancing productivity clearly.

AI Client Management Tool	Clearly Explained Practical Benefits
Trello, Monday.com AI	Clearly organizes projects, tasks, automatic reminders
Notion AI, Asana	Practically structures client work, enhances organization clearly
Calendly, Grammarly AI	Clearly manages client meetings, professional communications practically

Clear practical scenario:

Managing multiple freelance projects? Notion AI clearly creates structured project plans instantly, practically organizes client tasks, and ensures clear progress tracking —simplifying your workflow significantly.

⚡ AI Tools for Freelancers Clearly Compared

Here's a clear comparison of exactly how AI practically helps freelancers with research, marketing, and client management:

Freelance Task Category	Clearly Explained AI Benefits	Recommended AI Tools
Research & Writing	Instant summaries, fact-checking, outlines clearly	ChatGPT, Perplexity, Notion AI
Marketing & Outreach	Clearly creates content, automates social media practically	Jasper AI, Buffer, Grammarly
Client Work Management	Clearly organizes tasks, manages communication practically	Trello AI, Notion AI, Calendly

▶ Common Misunderstandings Clearly Explained

Clearly clarifying myths about AI freelance tools:

- ✖ **Myth:** AI reduces originality or creativity in freelance work.

  ✅ **Reality:** AI clearly enhances creativity practically, providing initial drafts and ideas while freelancers refine with unique insights.

- ✖ **Myth:** AI automation reduces personal client relationships.

  ✅ **Reality:** AI clearly supports personalized client interactions practically, enhancing professional communication consistently.

- ❌ **Myth:** AI research and fact-checking tools are unreliable.

  ✅ **Reality:** AI clearly increases accuracy practically, instantly providing reliable, verified information clearly and quickly.

📋 **Quick Summary Table: AI for Freelancers Clearly Summarized**

Freelance Task	Clearly Explained Practical AI Benefits	Recommended AI Tools
Research & Content Creation	Clearly saves time, provides instant accurate research	ChatGPT, Perplexity AI
Marketing & Client Outreach	Clearly automates content, social media, professional messaging	Jasper AI, Buffer, Grammarly
Client Project Management	Clearly organizes tasks, communication, project timelines practically	Trello, Notion AI, Calendly

📝 **Why AI Clearly Matters for Freelancers**

Clearly integrating AI tools practically enhances your freelance career, productivity, and professional success:

- **Increased Productivity:**
  AI clearly automates research, marketing, and client management practically, saving hours of manual work weekly.

- **Professional Quality and Efficiency:**
  AI practically ensures professional-quality

communication, content, and project management clearly and consistently.

- **Reduced Stress and Workload:**
  AI clearly simplifies freelance tasks practically, reducing stress and freeing your focus for meaningful, creative work.

Simply put, AI tools clearly enable freelancers to work faster, smarter, and more professionally—dramatically simplifying freelance success practically.

⬤ Small Business Tools: Branding, Ads, and Customer Support

Running a small business is rewarding but demanding—especially when managing branding, marketing campaigns, and customer support. Artificial Intelligence (AI) clearly simplifies these tasks practically, enabling you to build your brand effectively, create compelling advertisements, and deliver outstanding customer support effortlessly.

In this chapter, we'll clearly explore exactly how AI practically enhances small business branding, advertising, and customer interactions. You'll discover practical AI tools clearly designed to streamline business operations, attract more customers, and grow your brand successfully.

◎ AI for Branding: Build Your Business Identity Effortlessly

Branding clearly defines your business identity, influencing customer perception and loyalty. AI-powered branding tools practically help small businesses quickly create professional logos, brand visuals, and consistent messaging clearly, without costly marketing agencies.

Exactly how AI clearly simplifies small business branding practically:

- **Instant Logo and Brand Design:**
  AI clearly generates professional, customized logos and branding materials exactly tailored to your business identity instantly and affordably.

- **Consistent Brand Messaging:**
  AI practically ensures clear, consistent branding across websites, social media, and marketing materials—helping your small business build a strong, recognizable presence clearly.

- **Market Research and Brand Positioning:**
  AI instantly analyzes competitors, customer preferences, and market trends clearly, practically guiding your brand positioning effectively and quickly.

AI Branding Tool	Clearly Explained Practical Benefits
Looka, Brandmark	Instantly creates professional logos and branding clearly
Tailor Brands	Clearly ensures consistent branding, marketing practically
Canva AI	Practically generates professional visuals instantly

Clear practical scenario:

Need a professional logo fast? Looka AI clearly generates multiple logo options instantly, exactly customized to your small business brand—practically giving you a polished, professional look quickly.

📣 AI for Ads: Effective Marketing Made Easy

Creating effective advertisements clearly attracts customers and boosts sales—but ads can be costly and complicated. AI-powered advertising tools practically simplify ad creation, targeting, and optimization clearly, ensuring maximum effectiveness at minimal effort and cost.

Exactly how AI clearly improves small business advertising practically:

- **Instant Ad Creation:**
  AI practically generates engaging, professional ad copy, visuals, and headlines clearly tailored exactly to your target audience—simplifying ad creation significantly.

- **Precise Audience Targeting:**
  AI clearly identifies and targets potential customers practically based on behaviors, interests, and demographics—ensuring your ads reach the right audience instantly.

- **Automated Ad Optimization:**
  AI clearly tests and refines ads automatically, practically optimizing campaigns instantly to improve results and maximize your advertising budget effectively.

AI Advertising Tool	Clearly Explained Practical Benefits
AdCreative.ai, Jasper AI	Instantly creates compelling ads clearly and professionally
Meta Ads AI (Facebook)	Clearly targets audiences, optimizes ads practically
Google Ads AI	Practically automates ad targeting, clear campaign optimization

Clear practical example:

Creating social media ads? AdCreative.ai clearly generates multiple engaging ad options instantly, practically optimized exactly to attract your target customers effectively and affordably.

📞 AI for Customer Support: Exceptional Service Effortlessly

Outstanding customer support clearly strengthens loyalty and grows small businesses. AI-powered customer support tools practically automate interactions, improve response times, and enhance customer experiences clearly —without hiring expensive support teams.

Exactly how AI practically simplifies customer support clearly:

- **24/7 AI Chatbots:**
  AI clearly handles customer inquiries instantly, practically providing immediate answers and reducing your support workload significantly.

- **Personalized Customer Interactions:**
  AI clearly delivers personalized customer experiences practically, remembering customer preferences, histories, and proactively suggesting helpful solutions.

- **Automated Issue Resolution:**
  AI practically identifies common customer issues instantly, clearly providing automatic solutions and freeing your team for more complex tasks.

AI Customer Support Tool	Clearly Explained Practical Benefits
Intercom, Drift AI	Clearly automates customer interactions instantly
Zendesk AI, Freshdesk AI	Practically handles customer issues clearly, personalized responses
Tidio AI	Clearly provides immediate, automated customer support practically

Clear practical scenario:

Customers frequently ask similar questions. Drift AI chatbot clearly and practically handles these instantly, providing consistent, professional support 24/7—clearly improving customer satisfaction without additional staff.

⚡ AI Tools for Small Businesses Clearly Compared

Here's a clear comparison exactly showing how AI practically helps small businesses across branding, advertising, and customer support:

Small Business Task	Clearly Explained AI Benefits	Recommended AI Tools
Branding & Identity	Instantly creates professional branding clearly	Looka, Brandmark, Canva AI
Advertising & Marketing	Practically generates targeted, optimized ads clearly	AdCreative.ai, Meta Ads AI, Jasper AI
Customer Support	Clearly automates interactions practically	Intercom AI, Zendesk AI, Drift AI

▶ Common Misunderstandings Clearly Explained

Clearly clarifying myths about AI small business tools:

- ✖ **Myth:** AI-generated branding feels impersonal or generic.

  ✅ **Reality:** AI practically customizes branding exactly to your business identity clearly, creating professional, personalized results instantly.

135

- ❌ **Myth:** AI advertising always requires large budgets.

  ✅ **Reality:** AI practically optimizes small-budget ads clearly, targeting precisely and affordably for small business success effectively.

- ❌ **Myth:** AI customer support replaces human interactions completely.

  ✅ **Reality:** AI clearly handles routine inquiries practically, enhancing support quality, while complex issues remain handled personally.

📋 Quick Summary Table: AI for Small Businesses Clearly Summarized

Business Task	Clearly Explained Practical AI Benefits	Recommended AI Tools
Branding & Visual Identity	Clearly creates professional branding instantly	Looka, Tailor Brands, Canva AI
Advertising & Promotion	Clearly generates effective, optimized ads practically	AdCreative.ai, Google Ads AI, Jasper AI
Customer Support & Service	Clearly automates support, enhances customer satisfaction practically	Intercom, Zendesk, Tidio AI

📝 Why AI Clearly Matters for Small Businesses

Clearly integrating AI practically transforms your small business operations, marketing, and customer experience:

- **Affordable Professionalism:**
  AI clearly provides professional branding, ads, and customer support practically, without large budgets or staffing costs.

- **Enhanced Efficiency:**
  AI practically automates tasks clearly, significantly reducing workloads and increasing productivity instantly.

- **Improved Customer Experience:**
  AI clearly delivers exceptional, personalized interactions practically, growing customer loyalty effortlessly.

Simply put, AI clearly helps small businesses succeed practically—simplifying operations, enhancing branding, and improving customer experiences instantly and affordably.

● AI in Hiring and HR: The Future of Workflows

Managing hiring and human resources (HR) can quickly become overwhelming—sifting through resumes, scheduling interviews, and handling employee onboarding takes considerable time and effort. Artificial Intelligence (AI) clearly simplifies and streamlines these processes practically, transforming HR workflows, reducing bias, and improving hiring outcomes effectively.

In this chapter, we'll clearly explore exactly how AI practically enhances HR efficiency, simplifies hiring, and supports better employee management—helping your organization save time, improve diversity, and create a more productive workplace effortlessly.

AI for Recruitment: Faster, Fairer Hiring

Finding the right candidate clearly involves reviewing countless resumes, scheduling interviews, and making unbiased hiring decisions. AI-powered recruitment tools practically automate these tasks clearly, significantly speeding up hiring while enhancing fairness and objectivity.

Exactly how AI clearly simplifies recruitment practically:

- **Automatic Resume Screening:**
  AI practically analyzes resumes instantly, clearly identifying top candidates based on skills, experience, and qualifications—eliminating manual sorting and reducing human bias clearly.

- **Smart Interview Scheduling:**
  AI automatically schedules interviews practically, instantly managing calendars, sending invitations clearly, and saving HR professionals substantial time.

- **Unbiased Candidate Selection:**
  AI clearly assesses applicants practically using consistent criteria, promoting objective hiring decisions clearly and effectively reducing unconscious bias.

AI Recruitment Tool	Clearly Explained Practical Benefits
HireVue, Pymetrics	Clearly automates screening practically, reduces hiring bias
Calendly, Clara AI	Instantly schedules interviews, simplifies coordination practically
LinkedIn Recruiter AI	Clearly identifies qualified candidates practically, streamlines sourcing

Clear practical scenario:

You receive hundreds of resumes. AI clearly screens these instantly, practically identifying the top ten candidates exactly matching your requirements—reducing weeks of manual review clearly to just minutes.

📅 AI for Employee Onboarding: Efficient and Organized

Onboarding new employees clearly requires significant paperwork, training, and orientation tasks. AI-powered onboarding tools practically automate these processes clearly, creating efficient, organized onboarding experiences instantly for both HR teams and new hires.

Exactly how AI practically simplifies employee onboarding clearly:

- **Automated Paperwork and Documentation:** AI clearly manages new-hire documentation instantly, practically completing forms and processing required paperwork automatically and accurately.

- **Personalized Training Plans:** AI clearly creates personalized training programs practically tailored exactly to each employee's role, skills, and experience—accelerating productivity quickly.

- **Smart Onboarding Communication:** AI clearly sends automatic reminders and updates practically, ensuring new hires clearly understand processes, timelines, and expectations—enhancing satisfaction and engagement.

AI Onboarding Tool	Clearly Explained Practical Benefits
BambooHR AI, Workday AI	Clearly automates paperwork practically, personalizes training plans
Trello AI, ClickUp AI	Practically manages onboarding tasks clearly, enhances organization
Enboarder AI	Clearly communicates onboarding clearly, improves employee engagement practically

Clear practical example:

New hires receive automatic welcome emails, clearly personalized onboarding schedules, and instant reminders practically—ensuring smooth transitions, reduced confusion, and quicker employee integration clearly.

AI for Employee Management: Productivity and Engagement

Effectively managing employees clearly involves tracking performance, supporting development, and promoting engagement. AI-powered employee management tools practically simplify these tasks clearly, boosting productivity, improving retention, and enhancing workplace satisfaction practically.

Exactly how AI clearly improves employee management practically:

- **Real-Time Performance Insights:**
  AI practically monitors performance clearly, providing instant insights exactly identifying areas of strength and improvement—guiding personalized employee development clearly and effectively.

- **Proactive Engagement and Retention:**
  AI clearly detects signs of low engagement practically, automatically recommending strategies clearly to improve satisfaction and retention proactively.

- **Automated Employee Feedback:**
  AI practically collects and analyzes employee feedback clearly, instantly identifying issues, improving communication practically, and enhancing workplace culture clearly.

AI Employee Management Tool	Clearly Explained Practical Benefits
Culture Amp, Lattice AI	Clearly measures performance practically, improves employee engagement
15Five AI	Clearly collects real-time feedback practically, improves workplace culture
Betterworks AI	Clearly supports goal-setting practically, boosts productivity instantly

Clear practical scenario:

AI clearly identifies declining employee engagement instantly. Practically, it recommends targeted solutions exactly to boost motivation and satisfaction clearly—improving overall team performance effectively.

⚡ AI in Hiring and HR Clearly Compared

Here's a clear comparison exactly showing how AI practically transforms hiring and HR workflows:

HR Workflow	Clearly Explained AI Benefits	Recommended AI Tools
Recruitment & Hiring	Clearly automates candidate selection, reduces bias practically	HireVue, Pymetrics, LinkedIn Recruiter AI
Onboarding & Training	Clearly automates paperwork, personalizes training practically	BambooHR, Enboarder, Trello AI
Employee Engagement & Management	Clearly monitors performance, proactively improves engagement practically	Culture Amp, Lattice AI, 15Five AI

▶ Common Misunderstandings Clearly Explained

Clearly clarifying myths about AI in HR workflows:

- ✖ **Myth:** AI recruitment removes human judgment entirely.

  ✅ **Reality:** AI clearly supports human decisions practically, objectively screening candidates, while final decisions remain human-driven.

- ✖ **Myth:** AI onboarding feels impersonal or overwhelming to new hires.

  ✅ **Reality:** AI clearly personalizes onboarding practically, providing organized, welcoming experiences exactly tailored to each employee.

- ✖ **Myth:** AI management tools create mistrust or surveillance culture.

  ✅ **Reality:** AI practically enhances transparency and communication clearly, supporting positive employee relationships effectively.

📋 Quick Summary Table: AI in Hiring and HR Clearly Summarized

HR Task	Clearly Explained Practical AI Benefits	Recommended AI Tools
Recruitment & Candidate Selection	Clearly reduces bias, automates processes practically	HireVue, Calendly AI, LinkedIn Recruiter AI
Employee Onboarding & Training	Clearly automates onboarding, personalizes training practically	BambooHR, Enboarder, ClickUp AI
Employee Performance & Engagement	Clearly tracks performance, boosts engagement practically	Culture Amp, 15Five AI, Betterworks AI

Why AI Clearly Matters for Hiring and HR

Clearly integrating AI practically transforms hiring and HR workflows—significantly enhancing efficiency, reducing bias, and improving workplace productivity and satisfaction instantly:

- **Faster, Fairer Hiring:**
  AI clearly automates candidate screening practically, saving time and improving objectivity clearly.

- **Efficient, Personalized Onboarding:**
  AI clearly streamlines onboarding practically, improving new hire satisfaction and productivity instantly.

- **Enhanced Employee Engagement:**
  AI practically supports employee management clearly, proactively improving performance and workplace culture effectively.

Simply put, AI clearly empowers HR teams practically—simplifying complex processes, improving hiring outcomes, and enhancing employee experiences instantly and effectively.

AI for Solopreneurs: Build Your Brand with Less Stress

Being a solopreneur means doing it all—marketing, client communication, product creation, branding, and more. While this independence is empowering, it also brings a heavy workload. Thankfully, Artificial Intelligence (AI) clearly lightens the load, practically helping you work smarter, automate tasks, and grow your brand efficiently —without burnout.

In this chapter, we'll clearly explore exactly how AI supports solopreneurs by simplifying brand-building, streamlining daily operations, and freeing time for meaningful, creative work. You'll discover practical tools to build a strong, recognizable brand with less stress and more clarity.

AI for Branding: Build Your Identity with Ease

Your brand is your business identity. As a solopreneur, you need a consistent and professional look across all platforms—but creating one from scratch can be time-consuming and costly. AI-powered branding tools clearly simplify the entire process, helping you launch confidently without hiring a designer or agency.

Exactly how AI practically supports branding for solopreneurs:

- **Logo and Visual Creation:**
  AI tools like **Looka** and **Tailor Brands** instantly generate professional logos, brand colors, fonts, and even full brand kits tailored clearly to your business niche and preferences.

145

- **Personalized Style Guides:**
  AI clearly builds consistent visual styles—perfect for social media, websites, packaging, or presentations—ensuring your brand looks polished and memorable across all platforms.

- **Market Positioning and Voice:**
  AI analyzes similar businesses clearly, helping you identify how to stand out, refine your messaging, and define a clear brand voice that connects emotionally with your audience.

AI Branding Tool	Clearly Explained Practical Benefits
Looka	Instantly creates logos and brand kits clearly
Tailor Brands	Complete brand identity platform, personalized
Canva AI	Easily creates branded visuals and social posts

Clear practical scenario:

You're launching a digital course. Looka AI instantly creates a custom logo, color palette, and branded templates clearly aligned with your audience—saving hours of design work practically.

📈 AI for Business Growth: Automate and Expand with Confidence

Solopreneurs often wear every hat in the business—from marketing to customer service. AI helps reduce that pressure, practically automating repetitive tasks so you can focus clearly on growth and innovation.

Exactly how AI helps grow your solo business practically:

- **Content Creation Made Simple:**
  AI tools like **Jasper** or **ChatGPT** create blog posts, social captions, ad copy, and email sequences instantly—clearly freeing you from writing fatigue while ensuring consistent messaging.

- **Smart Scheduling and Organization:**
  AI clearly manages your time, calendars, and to-dos with tools like **Motion** or **Reclaim.ai**, helping you stay focused, avoid burnout, and maintain a healthy work-life balance.

- **Marketing & Customer Funnels:**
  AI powers email campaigns, lead scoring, and social ad optimization—clearly turning solo effort into scalable systems that work around the clock.

AI Growth Tool	Clearly Explained Practical Benefits
Jasper AI	Instantly creates marketing content clearly
Reclaim.ai	Auto-schedules work blocks, breaks, and tasks
ConvertKit + AI	Builds email funnels, segments audiences smartly

Clear practical example:

You're preparing a product launch. Jasper AI writes your landing page copy, ConvertKit sets up the email series, and Reclaim.ai schedules your daily workflow—clearly helping you launch like a team of five.

💬 AI for Communication: Speak Like a Pro, Work Like a Team

Even if you're working solo, your communication needs to sound professional—whether you're writing proposals, replying to customers, or creating social posts. AI tools clearly improve how you communicate, helping you stay organized, consistent, and confident.

Exactly how AI practically improves solopreneur communication:

- **Professional Messaging:**
  AI clearly helps draft polished, on-brand emails, pitches, and responses with tools like **Grammarly** or **ChatGPT**, ensuring clarity and confidence in every message.

- **Client & Lead Management:**
  AI CRMs like **Bonsai** or **Zoho CRM** automate follow-ups, proposal templates, and even invoicing —clearly freeing you to focus on delivering value.

- **Social Engagement:**
  AI social tools instantly generate captions, schedule content, and track engagement clearly—keeping your audience engaged even when you're offline.

AI Communication Tool	Clearly Explained Practical Benefits
Grammarly	Enhances tone, grammar, and clarity instantly
Bonsai (with AI)	Manages proposals, contracts, and client workflows
Buffer AI / Later AI	Schedules and generates social content efficiently

Clear practical scenario:

A client emails you a last-minute question. Grammarly suggests a professional, warm reply instantly. Meanwhile, Buffer AI schedules your week's social posts, and Bonsai sends your next invoice automatically.

⚡ The Solopreneur AI Stack – Clearly Compared

Task Area	AI Tools to Use Clearly and Practically	Key Benefits
Branding & Visual Identity	Looka, Tailor Brands, Canva AI	Create a professional brand instantly
Marketing & Content	Jasper, ConvertKit AI, ChatGPT	Scale content creation effortlessly
Time & Workflow	Reclaim.ai, Motion AI	Manage time and tasks clearly
Client Communication	Grammarly, Bonsai, Buffer AI	Stay polished and responsive

▶ Common Misunderstandings Clearly Explained

- ❌ **Myth:** Solopreneurs don't need AI—just more time.

  ✅ **Reality:** AI gives you that time, practically automating tasks that drain your energy daily.

- ❌ **Myth:** AI makes branding and marketing impersonal.

  ✅ **Reality:** AI clearly adapts to your voice, helping you maintain authenticity while working faster.

- ✖ **Myth:** AI tools are too complex or expensive for solo businesses.

  ✅ **Reality:** Many AI tools are affordable, easy to use, and designed exactly for small-scale entrepreneurs.

📝 Why AI Clearly Matters for Solopreneurs

Using AI in your solo business practically reduces workload, enhances professionalism, and enables consistent, scalable growth—without hiring a team.

- **Work Smarter, Not Harder:**
  AI clearly handles repetitive tasks so you focus on strategy, service, and creativity.

- **Boost Your Brand:**
  AI helps build a professional, recognizable brand clearly and quickly.

- **Deliver More with Less Stress:**
  AI enables smooth communication, clean workflows, and consistent output—without overwork.

Simply put, AI empowers solopreneurs to act like full teams—building brands, running operations, and serving clients with less stress and more clarity.

SECTION 4

CREATIVE AND PERSONAL
EXPRESSION THROUGH AI

(Exploring your creative side — even if you're "not creative")

Creating Art with AI: Midjourney, DALL·E and More

Art is no longer limited to those who can draw or paint. Today, Artificial Intelligence (AI) allows anyone— regardless of skill level—to create beautiful, imaginative, and even professional-looking artwork using simple text prompts. Whether you're exploring creativity for fun or trying to visualize a business idea, AI art tools like **Midjourney**, **DALL·E**, and others clearly open the door to a whole new world of creative expression.

In this chapter, we'll clearly explore exactly how you can use AI tools to create digital art, illustrations, concepts, and visual ideas—just by describing what you want to see. Even if you've never made art before, AI makes the process fun, easy, and surprisingly powerful.

What Is AI-Generated Art (Clearly Explained)?

AI art is created by software that understands your written instructions (called prompts) and turns them into visual images. You don't need to draw, choose colors, or use complicated tools. You just type what you imagine—and the AI creates it for you.

Exactly how AI art tools work:

1 **You write a prompt** like:
   "A futuristic city in the clouds at sunset, glowing buildings, flying cars."

2 **The AI processes the words**, understands your meaning, and searches for patterns in its training data (millions of real artworks, photos, and styles).

3 **It generates an image** that visually represents what you described—often in less than a minute.

The result? A high-quality digital image that feels like it came from a professional designer or concept artist.

🐾 Popular AI Art Tools Clearly Compared

Tool Name	What It Does Best	Accessibility
Midjou rney	Highly artistic, detailed, stylized illustrations	Discord-based, subscription required
DALL· E	Realistic and creative images, open to all	Web-based, free tier on OpenAI
Craiyo n	Simple, quick images for fun or concept sketching	Free, web-based
NightC afe	Abstract and photorealistic styles, community hub	Free and paid options

Clear practical scenario:

You're designing a book cover or brainstorming product packaging. You type:
"A cozy mountain cabin at night, glowing windows, snow falling softly, moon in the sky."
Midjourney instantly generates four variations of beautiful, atmospheric images you can use or refine.

🧠 AI as a Visual Brainstorming Partner

Even if you're not an artist, you can think like a designer. AI tools help visualize your ideas, explore variations, and bring creative thoughts to life visually.

Ways solopreneurs and creatives use AI art practically:

- **Logo concepts and brand moodboards**

- **Social media post backgrounds**

- **Children's book illustrations**

- **Product design mockups**

- **Fantasy or sci-fi concept art**

AI lets you test styles, colors, and layouts visually before committing to a designer—clearly saving time and money.

Prompt Examples: What You Can Say to AI

You don't need to be technical to talk to AI art generators. Just describe what you want to see, like you're explaining it to a friend.

Basic prompts:

- *"A magical forest with glowing trees and fireflies"*

- *"An old pirate ship sailing through a thunderstorm"*

Advanced prompts (to guide style):

- *"A watercolor painting of a small bakery at sunset, warm light inside"*

- *"Cyberpunk city street in the rain, digital neon signs, in the style of Blade Runner"*

AI understands emotion, mood, color, composition—even art styles like Picasso, Van Gogh, anime, or pixel art.

✒️ Tips for Better AI Artwork (Prompt Crafting Basics)

Creating great art with AI is a skill you can improve. Here are some practical tips:

- **Be specific.**
  "A dog" will give you a generic image.
  "A golden retriever puppy wearing a red scarf, sitting in a snowy park" gives you magic.

- **Add style or medium.**
  Try phrases like *"oil painting," "digital art," "photorealistic," "cartoon," "low-poly 3D,"* etc.

- **Use modifiers.**
  Words like *soft lighting, moody atmosphere, high detail, fantasy style* change the tone of your image.

- **Explore variations.**
  Most platforms let you regenerate or tweak results. Try multiple versions and save your favorites.

🚀 Who Uses AI Art in Real Life?

- **Entrepreneurs** create product mockups, marketing graphics, and logo drafts.

- **Authors** generate book covers, character art, and chapter illustrations.

- **Teachers** visualize classroom materials or concepts.

- **Designers** brainstorm faster and explore new styles.

- **Everyday people** turn imagination into wallpapers, posters, gifts, or hobbies.

AI art isn't just for artists—it's for anyone with ideas.

📋 Quick Summary Table: AI Art Use Cases Clearly Explained

Use Case	How AI Helps Practically	Recommended Tool
Branding & Logos	Rapid visual drafts and concept testing	Looka, DALL·E, Midjourney
Book or Blog Illustrations	High-quality, style-specific visuals	Midjourney, NightCafe
Product Design & Packaging	Concept visuals and style moodboards	DALL·E, Canva AI
Fun & Personal Projects	Posters, digital art, gifts	Craiyon, NightCafe

Music and Sound Creation: AI as Your Studio Partner

You don't need instruments, a studio, or formal training to create music anymore. With Artificial Intelligence (AI), anyone—yes, even you—can compose songs, beats, soundtracks, or ambient sounds using just ideas and prompts. Whether you're a creator, business owner, teacher, or simply curious, AI music tools let you express yourself musically, clearly and easily.

In this chapter, we'll clearly explore how AI-powered music platforms help you generate melodies, build full tracks, experiment with genres, and even produce podcast intros or social media sounds—all without needing to read sheet music or touch an instrument.

What Is AI Music Creation? (Clearly Explained)

AI music tools analyze thousands of musical patterns, genres, and structures. Based on your input—like mood, tempo, instruments, or even written lyrics—they generate original music, adapting to your style or purpose.

Exactly how AI creates music:

1   **You choose or describe the mood, genre, or instruments.**
    Example: *"Calm background music with piano and strings for meditation"*

2   **The AI composes a track**—melody, harmony, rhythm—based on your input.

3   You can edit, rearrange, or export the result for
use in videos, podcasts, social posts, or just for fun.

The music is royalty-free and ready to use anywhere—no
licensing hassles.

🎼 Popular AI Music Tools Clearly Compared

Tool Name	Best For	Accessibility
Soundraw	Creating tracks for videos, ads, and content	Subscription-based, intuitive UI
AIVA	Composing cinematic, classical, or ambient music	Web-based, free and paid options
Amper Music	Simple drag-and-drop music creation	Cloud-based, royalty-free output
Boomy	Making songs with vocals and lyrics	Beginner-friendly, fast publishing
LALAL. AI	Isolating vocals or instruments from tracks	Audio processing for remixes

Clear practical scenario:

You're making a YouTube video or a meditation app.
Using **AIVA**, you create a soft ambient piano piece in 30
seconds—ready to export and use, no studio needed.

🧠 AI as Your Musical Brainstorm Partner

Even if you're not a musician, you can think like one. AI
tools act like a virtual composer—quickly offering
variations, styles, and sounds based on your vision.

How creators use AI music practically:

- **Small businesses** generate theme music for brand videos.

- **YouTubers and podcasters** create intros, transitions, and mood tracks.

- **Educators** build background sounds for courses or learning tools.

- **Writers** generate custom soundtracks for books, poems, or storytelling.

- **Casual users** explore musical creativity and share songs with friends.

🎹 Prompt Examples: What You Can Ask AI Music Tools

Depending on the tool, you can select from menus or write a short instruction. Here's how to clearly guide the AI:

By genre or purpose:

- *"Electronic dance music with a fast beat for a workout video"*

- *"Lo-fi hip hop with rain sounds for background focus music"*

By emotion or mood:

- *"Melancholic piano and cello duet for a short film"*

- *"Uplifting acoustic guitar with claps and drums for a commercial"*

By structure:

- *"Intro – slow build, Chorus – energetic, Outro – fade"*

- *"60-second track with rise and fall for ad background"*

🛠 Editing and Customizing Your Music

Most AI tools allow you to:

- Adjust **tempo**, **instrument types**, and **duration**

- Loop or cut sections to fit your project

- Layer melodies, harmonies, and beats

- Export files in formats like MP3, WAV, or MIDI

Some (like **Boomy**) even let you add lyrics and AI vocals, producing full tracks in pop, hip-hop, or electronic styles.

🚀 Who's Using AI Music Tools in Real Life?

- **Startups** add custom music to pitch decks, branding, or explainer videos.

- **Freelancers** create affordable music for clients without needing a composer.

- **Game developers** generate ambient loops or action themes for small titles.

- **Podcasters** design intros, outros, and background loops without hiring musicians.

- **Hobbyists** make entire songs and publish them to Spotify through tools like Boomy.

📋 Quick Summary Table: AI Music Creation Clearly Explained

Use Case	AI Tools That Help Practically	Benefit
Background music for content	Soundraw, AIVA, Amper	Custom-fit music in minutes
Full songs with vocals	Boomy, Loudly AI	AI writes lyrics, adds vocal style
Audio editing/ remixing	LALAL.AI, Moises.ai	Separate voice and instruments easily
Teaching or storytelling	AIVA, Amadeus Code	Create narrative-enhancing soundtracks

▶ Common Misunderstandings Clearly Explained

- ❌ **Myth:** AI music sounds robotic or fake.

  ✅ **Reality:** AI-generated music today is rich, emotive, and often indistinguishable from human compositions.

- ❌ **Myth:** You must be a musician to use these tools.

  ✅ **Reality:** AI handles the technical work. You just bring ideas or moods—it's as easy as selecting options or writing a sentence.

- ❌ **Myth:** AI music isn't legal to use.

  ✅ **Reality:** Most tools create royalty-free music you can use in podcasts, videos, games, or commercials without licensing issues.

161

⬤ Write Your First Poem, Song, or Short Story With AI

Creative writing may seem like something only poets, lyricists, or novelists do—but with Artificial Intelligence (AI), it becomes approachable, fun, and completely accessible. Whether you're crafting your first poem, curious about writing lyrics, or want to experiment with fiction, AI tools can help you overcome creative blocks, generate ideas, and bring your words to life.

In this chapter, we'll clearly explore how AI supports your creative expression—step by step. You'll see how to use tools like **ChatGPT**, **Sudowrite**, and **Rytr** to create poetry, songs, and short stories, even if you've never written creatively before.

✎ Why Use AI for Creative Writing?

Writing is powerful—but it can also feel intimidating. AI makes the blank page less scary by giving you instant suggestions, helping you shape your ideas, and offering creative phrasing that sparks inspiration.

Exactly how AI helps you write creatively:

- **Generates first drafts quickly** so you can start without pressure.

- **Offers multiple variations** of poems, verses, or scenes to explore tone and style.

- **Improves flow, rhythm, and word choice** so your writing feels natural and polished.

- **Completes your sentences or stanzas** when you get stuck—like a helpful creative partner.

🧠 AI Tools for Creative Writing – Clearly Compared

Tool Name	Best For	Key Feature
ChatGPT	General writing (poems, songs, fiction)	Versatile, interactive idea generator
Sudowrite	Fiction and storytelling	Descriptive enhancements, plot suggestions
Rytr	Short-form content, lyrics	Fast drafts, tone control
Jasper AI	Blog posts, poetry, SEO writing	Creative + commercial writing support
Verse by Verse	Poetry inspired by classic poets	Offers poetic lines in historic styles

Clear practical scenario:

You want to write a love poem but don't know where to begin. You ask:
"Write a four-line romantic poem in the style of Robert Frost."
ChatGPT gives you several options instantly, and you pick the one that fits your tone best.

🎵 Writing Songs and Lyrics with AI

AI can help you write full song lyrics, from choruses to verses, and even suggest rhymes or melodies (if paired with music tools).

Prompt examples:

- *"Write lyrics for a hopeful pop song about new beginnings"*

- *"Give me a sad country ballad about lost love with a simple rhyme scheme"*

- *"Create a rap verse about working hard and chasing dreams"*

Most tools will follow the requested structure, tone, and style—instantly.

Bonus tip: You can pair the lyrics with AI music tools like **Boomy** or **Soundraw** to turn them into real songs.

📖 **Writing Short Stories with AI**

Short fiction is a fantastic way to explore creativity. AI helps with:

- **Story starters** and character ideas

- **Dialogue and descriptions**

- **Plot development**

- **Scene-by-scene generation**

Prompt examples:

- *"Write the first paragraph of a mystery story set in a snowy mountain village."*

- *"Describe a fantasy world where animals talk and the sky changes color every hour."*

AI can build your story with as much detail as you want—paragraph by paragraph or all at once. You stay in control of the plot.

AI and Structure: Poems, Songs, Stories

AI understands basic writing structures and can follow them easily:

Format	Common Structure AI Can Follow
Poem	Rhymed or free verse, haiku, limerick, sonnet
Song	Verse – Chorus – Verse – Bridge – Chorus
Story	Introduction – Conflict – Climax – Resolution

You can ask the AI to stick to specific formats or simply guide it by saying things like:
"Make it sound like a folk tale" or *"Use simple language for children."*

Tips for Great Creative Prompts

- **Start with a mood or theme:**
  "A peaceful poem about the ocean"
  "A horror story set in a quiet suburban neighborhood"

- **Add tone or emotion:**
  "Hopeful," "melancholy," "funny," "tense"

- **Guide the structure:**
  "Make it 3 verses, with an ABAB rhyme pattern"
  "Write a short story under 200 words"

- **Iterate:**
  Ask the AI: *"Make this more dramatic," "Add a twist at the end,"* or *"Rewrite it in simpler words."*

Who Uses AI for Creative Writing?

- **Teachers and students** use it for poetry lessons and storytelling exercises.

- **Musicians** create lyrics and song drafts for demos.

- **Bloggers and content creators** add unique quotes or poetic touches to articles.

- **Writers** use AI as a first-draft generator or brainstorming partner.

- **Everyday people** write personal poems, short stories, and social media captions just for fun.

Quick Summary Table: AI in Creative Writing

Writing Type	AI Can Help You With...	Recommended Tools
Poetry	Rhymes, imagery, structure, tone	ChatGPT, Verse by Verse
Songwriting	Lyrics, chorus ideas, rhyming patterns	ChatGPT, Rytr, Jasper
Short Stories	Plot, characters, dialogue, scenes	Sudowrite, ChatGPT
Personal Expression	Letters, quotes, social posts	ChatGPT, Rytr

▶ Common Misunderstandings Clearly Explained

- ❌ **Myth:** AI makes your writing less authentic.

  ✅ **Reality:** AI gives you ideas—you guide the voice. You still own the creativity.

- ❌ **Myth:** AI can't write in a specific style or tone.

  ✅ **Reality:** AI can match styles—classic poets, modern lyrics, or simple language—just tell it what you want.

- ❌ **Myth:** Only professional writers benefit from this.

  ✅ **Reality:** Beginners, hobbyists, and everyday users often benefit the most—it's a tool to help you start.

⬤ Design a Logo or Brand with Just Prompts

Creating a logo or developing a brand identity used to require graphic design skills or hiring a professional. But now, Artificial Intelligence (AI) tools make it possible to build a clean, professional, and fully customized brand using nothing but a few written prompts. Whether you're starting a new project, launching a business, or refreshing your personal look, AI helps you do it quickly, affordably, and clearly—without creative stress.

In this chapter, we'll clearly explore how you can design logos, define brand colors and fonts, and even build visual templates for your website or social media using AI tools —just by describing your idea.

◎ What Does AI Branding Really Do? (Clearly Explained)

AI branding tools analyze millions of existing logos, color combinations, typefaces, and visual styles. Based on your input—like business name, industry, mood, and style preferences—they generate a complete brand identity automatically.

Exactly what AI can generate for you:

- Logos (with icons, wordmarks, or both)
- Color palettes
- Font pairings
- Brand guidelines (when to use each element)

- Business card and social media templates

- Website mockups or launch-ready pages

And you can do all this with **no design background at all.**

🛠 Popular AI Tools for Logo and Brand Design

Tool Name	Best For	Key Features
Looka	Logo + full brand kit	AI-generated logo, brand colors, font suggestions
Tailor Brands	Small businesses, personal brands	Logo, website builder, branded merch tools
Brandm ark	Instant logo generation	Simple, clean designs with fast previews
Canva AI	Visual content creation + customization	Branded templates for social, slides, and more

Clear practical scenario:

You're launching a coaching business. You go to Looka, enter your business name and keywords like *"growth, calm, trust,"* and choose a modern style. In seconds, you see 10+ logo options, a complete color palette, and matching fonts—ready to use online and offline.

💡 How to Prompt AI to Design Your Brand

Most tools use step-by-step questions, but some also let you type free-form ideas. Here's how to get the best results:

Prompt elements to include:

- **Business or project name**

- **Industry or niche** (e.g. skincare, tech, education)

- **Tone or mood** (e.g. playful, elegant, minimal)

- **Keywords** that describe your mission or values

- **Color preferences** (optional)

Example input:

"My brand is called 'Little Roots.' It's a nature-inspired children's product line. I want a soft, earthy color palette, a handwritten-style font, and a simple logo featuring a plant or seedling. The brand should feel natural, gentle, and safe."

AI will instantly generate logos, show previews, and even create matching designs for Instagram, business cards, packaging, or your website.

🎨 Understanding the Brand Elements AI Provides

Brand Element	What It Means & Why It Matters
Logo	Your primary visual symbol—instantly recognizable
Color Palette	Defines the mood (e.g. trust = blue, energy = orange)
Typography	Communicates tone (e.g. serif = traditional, sans-serif = modern)
Brand Voice	Often suggested by AI based on keywords (friendly, bold, expert)
Templates	Social posts, business cards, slides that follow your brand style

AI gives you all of these instantly—and you can tweak them anytime.

⚡ Use Cases for AI-Generated Branding

- **Startups**: Build your visual identity before hiring a design team

- **Freelancers & Creators**: Create a personal brand that stands out

- **E-commerce Sellers**: Add polish to your packaging and online store

- **Nonprofits & Clubs**: Design consistent visuals for outreach or events

- **Side Projects**: Launch quickly with a cohesive look —even on a budget

✦ Tips for Better Results

- Be **clear and specific** about what you want: calm vs bold, fun vs elegant, traditional vs modern

- Choose 3–5 **keywords** that reflect your values or goals

- Don't be afraid to **regenerate** or **explore variations**—AI offers lots of styles

- Think about where you'll use your brand: Instagram? Packaging? Business cards?

▶ Common Misunderstandings Clearly Explained

- ❌ **Myth:** AI logos are generic or low quality

  ✅ **Reality:** AI tools today generate high-res, scalable designs that often rival agency work—especially for early-stage projects

- ❌ **Myth:** You still need Photoshop or Illustrator

  ✅ **Reality:** Most AI tools include easy-to-use editors and instant exports—no software required

- ❌ **Myth:** AI branding can't be unique

  ✅ **Reality:** You control the style, tone, and vision —AI is a fast, flexible assistant, not a one-size-fits-all engine

📋 Quick Summary Table: AI Branding for Non-Designers

Use Case	AI Tools That Help Practically	Result You Get
Starting a business	Looka, Tailor Brands	Full visual identity in minutes
Refreshing your image	Brandmark, Canva AI	New logo, updated colors and templates
Branding a product	Looka, Canva	Label designs, packaging visuals
Personal branding	Tailor Brands, Canva	Social media kits, bio pages, etc.

AI for Social Media Content Planning

Creating consistent, engaging content for social media can feel like a full-time job—especially when you're doing everything alone. But with Artificial Intelligence (AI), you can generate content ideas, write captions, plan a full month of posts, and even schedule everything across platforms… in a fraction of the time.

In this chapter, we'll clearly explore how AI tools help you brainstorm, write, design, and publish social media content easily and strategically. Whether you're a business owner, freelancer, content creator, or someone managing their personal brand, these tools can simplify your entire workflow—clearly and practically.

What AI Can Do for Social Media (Clearly Explained)

AI doesn't just write posts—it thinks ahead, understands trends, and adapts content to your audience, brand voice, and goals. With the right tools, AI becomes your:

- **Idea Generator** – Suggests content topics based on your niche, season, or audience

- **Copywriter** – Writes clear, engaging captions with hashtags, CTAs, and tone matching

- **Designer** – Suggests visuals or creates branded templates

- **Planner** – Builds a post calendar for daily/weekly/ monthly publishing

- **Scheduler** – Automatically queues posts across Instagram, Facebook, LinkedIn, and more

💼 Popular AI Tools for Social Media Planning

Tool Name	Best For	Key Features
Buffer + AI	Scheduling, caption writing	Post calendar, content suggestions, cross-posting
Later AI	Visual content planning	Drag & drop grid, auto-scheduling, analytics
Lately.ai	Repurposing long content	Turns blogs or videos into short social posts
Copy.ai	Fast, themed social media captions	Multiple styles and tones per post
Canva Magic Write	Designing visuals + writing captions	All-in-one design + text generation

Clear practical scenario:

You run a wellness coaching brand. Using **Later AI**, you plan your entire month of posts, **Copy.ai** writes your captions with the right tone and hashtags, and **Canva** creates branded graphics—all in just a few hours.

🧠 AI for Brainstorming Content Ideas

Not sure what to post? AI has you covered. Based on your niche, target audience, or platform, AI can suggest:

- Weekly themes (e.g. #MindsetMonday, #WellnessWednesday)

- Trending topics and hashtag challenges

- Holidays or awareness days to tie into your message

- Content types (polls, reels, behind-the-scenes, tips, testimonials)

Prompt examples:

- *"Give me 10 post ideas for a fitness coach on Instagram for April."*

- *"Suggest a weekly content plan for a handmade candle business."*

- *"What's trending on TikTok this week in mental health?"*

✍ AI for Writing Captions, Hashtags, and Hooks

Once you have your post ideas, AI can quickly generate polished, high-performing captions—tailored to the platform and your tone.

You can ask AI to:

- Write short or long captions

- Add emojis or leave them out

- Use casual, formal, funny, or inspirational tones

- Include calls to action (*"Click the link," "Share if you agree"*)

- Suggest relevant and trending hashtags

Prompt examples:

- *"Write an inspiring caption for a photo of a sunrise hike."*

- *"Create a caption for a business tip with 5 related hashtags."*

- *"Write a carousel caption in a confident tone for LinkedIn about personal growth."*

AI for Planning and Scheduling Posts

Once your content is created, AI-powered planners can:

- Build a full content calendar (daily, weekly, monthly)

- Auto-schedule posts at optimal times

- Adjust content across platforms (e.g. shorter for Twitter, longer for LinkedIn)

- Remind you when to engage with your audience

- Analyze what's working and suggest improvements

Tools like **Buffer**, **Later**, and **Planoly** integrate with AI writers to speed up the entire cycle—from draft to post.

Real-Life Use Cases

- **Freelancers** automate Instagram content to attract new clients

- **Small businesses** plan months of posts to promote products and build trust

- **Authors and coaches** post quotes, book excerpts, and testimonials consistently

- **Artists and makers** showcase work with minimal effort

- **Nonprofits** maintain awareness campaigns without a full media team

Quick Summary Table: AI for Social Media

Task	AI Tool That Helps Practically	Benefit
Post idea generation	ChatGPT, Copy.ai	No more "what should I post today?"
Caption writing	Copy.ai, Canva Magic Write	Posts that match tone and attract engagement
Visuals and graphics	Canva AI	Templates, carousels, infographics
Scheduling and automation	Later AI, Buffer, Planoly	Hands-off posting, cross-platform syncing
Repurposing long content	Lately.ai	Turn podcasts/blogs into 30+ micro-posts

Common Misunderstandings Clearly Explained

- **Myth:** AI makes your content sound robotic

  Reality: AI can match your tone—funny, professional, poetic, or casual—based on simple prompts

- **Myth:** Social media success requires being online all day

  Reality: AI lets you batch-plan weeks of posts in advance and automates scheduling

- ✖ **Myth:** You need to be an influencer to use these tools

  ✅ **Reality:** AI social planning tools help creators, educators, local shops, startups—anyone trying to stay consistent

⬤ Make Your Own Video Clips with AI Tools (Runway ML, Pictory)

Video is one of the most powerful ways to connect with an audience—but it's also one of the most time-consuming and intimidating to create. Thankfully, Artificial Intelligence (AI) tools now make video production accessible to anyone. No editing experience, no expensive software—just your ideas, and the AI does the rest.

In this chapter, we'll clearly explore how to create short-form videos, marketing clips, explainer videos, and social reels using AI platforms like **Runway ML** and **Pictory**. Whether you're a business owner, educator, or content creator, you'll learn how to bring your message to life—visually, quickly, and professionally.

🎬 What AI Video Tools Actually Do (Clearly Explained)

AI video tools combine automation, visual editing, and smart content generation to help you go from **idea to video** in just a few steps. Depending on the tool, AI can:

- Turn text (like blog posts or scripts) into full video clips

- Add voiceovers and subtitles automatically

- Select relevant stock footage and transitions

- Remove backgrounds or objects from video clips

- Enhance or animate video content with AI effects

Bottom line: AI reduces the time, skill, and stress required to make great videos.

Popular AI Video Creation Tools

Tool Name	Best For	Key Features
Pictory	Converting scripts or blog posts into videos	Auto-selects visuals, voiceovers, subtitles
Runway ML	Advanced video editing and effects	Background removal, motion tracking, AI video effects
Lumen5	Turning social captions into dynamic videos	Drag-and-drop editor + branded templates
InVideo	Quick marketing and explainer videos	Pre-made templates + AI assistance
Synthesia	AI-generated avatars for talking-head videos	Create spokesperson videos with just text

Clear practical scenario:

You have a blog post titled *"5 Tips for Better Sleep."* Pictory turns it into a 1-minute video with soft music, animated text, relevant images, and a natural-sounding AI voice—all in under 15 minutes.

 ## Use Cases for AI Video Tools

AI-powered video creation is perfect for:

- **Social media reels, shorts, and TikToks**
- **YouTube intro or educational clips**
- **Course content and online classes**
- **Explainer videos for products or services**
- **Ad creatives or sales promos**
- **Inspirational quote videos or story snippets**

And with templates and automatic formatting, you can match different platform sizes: square for Instagram, vertical for TikTok, landscape for YouTube.

✍ What You Can Give AI to Start a Video

You don't need video footage to begin. Just use:

- A **written script** (AI will match visuals + voice)

- A **blog post or article URL**

- A few **bullet points or tips**

- A **voiceover or audio file** (Runway or InVideo can sync visuals)

- A **text quote** or message you want animated

Prompt examples:

- *"Turn this list of fitness tips into a motivational video with upbeat music."*

- *"Create a 30-second explainer video about my coaching services using a confident tone."*

✒ AI Video Editing Features You'll Love

Feature	What It Does Clearly
Text-to-Video	Turns your writing into matching visuals + voice
Automatic Subtitles	Adds captions that improve accessibility & reach
Background Removal	Cleanly removes video backgrounds (Runway ML)
Voiceover Generation	AI reads your script in natural voices
Stock Footage Matching	Pulls relevant visuals automatically
Brand Customization	Adds your logo, fonts, and brand colors

◎ Who's Using AI Video Tools Right Now?

- **Startups** create ad campaigns and pitch videos

- **Teachers** record micro-lessons or course previews

- **Authors** turn quotes or summaries into book trailers

- **Influencers** repurpose blog posts into video content

- **Nonprofits** create low-cost awareness campaigns

- **Job seekers** make video resumes with Synthesia avatars

📋 Quick Summary Table: AI Video Creation

Goal	Recommended Tool(s)	Benefit You Get
Turn a script into a video	Pictory, InVideo	Professional video without editing skills
Add AI effects or edits to footage	Runway ML	Visual polish, object removal, animation
Create branded social clips	Lumen5, Canva Video	Easy templates, resize for any platform
Make avatar-based videos	Synthesia	Professional "presenter" videos with no filming

▶ Common Misunderstandings Clearly Explained

- ❌ **Myth:** You need a camera or footage to make videos

  ✅ **Reality:** AI uses text, images, or voice to create full videos from scratch

- ❌ **Myth:** AI videos look generic or low-quality

  ✅ **Reality:** With the right prompts and branding, AI creates clean, modern, scroll-stopping visuals

- ❌ **Myth:** You need a big budget to make good content

  ✅ **Reality:** Many tools are free or offer affordable plans for solo creators and small businesses

AI as Your Personal Coach or Brainstorm Partner

Sometimes, all you need is a second brain—someone (or something) to bounce ideas off, help you organize your thoughts, or motivate you when you're stuck. That's where Artificial Intelligence (AI) comes in—not just as a tool, but as a **personal coach**, **thinking partner**, or **creative companion**.

In this chapter, we'll clearly explore how AI can help you brainstorm, plan, reflect, and solve problems—whether you're making a big decision, building a new project, or just trying to get out of a creative rut. You don't need a mentor on call. With the right AI tools, you have 24/7 support.

What Does a "Personal AI Coach" Do? (Clearly Explained)

AI can guide you through thought processes, ask insightful questions, and even help you prioritize goals or reframe challenges. Depending on your need, it can be:

- A **career coach** (helping you plan next steps or improve your resume)

- A **creative partner** (generating story, product, or content ideas)

- A **decision assistant** (weighing pros and cons or clarifying options)

- A **wellness motivator** (tracking goals or helping build healthy habits)

184

- A **project planner** (breaking ideas into action steps and timelines)

All you need to do is ask, and AI responds clearly and supportively.

💬 Realistic Prompts You Can Try

Whether you're brainstorming or seeking advice, here's how to ask AI clearly:

✅ Personal Growth / Motivation:

- *"Help me set 3 realistic fitness goals for the next month."*

- *"Give me a morning routine that boosts focus and energy."*

- *"What are 5 small habits that improve confidence?"*

✅ Career Coaching:

- *"I'm feeling stuck at work—can you help me explore new directions?"*

- *"Suggest ways to improve my resume for a project manager role."*

- *"What are pros and cons of switching from a corporate job to freelancing?"*

✅ Brainstorming:

- *"Give me 10 unique product ideas for eco-friendly gifts."*

- *"I want to write a children's book—can you help brainstorm a plot?"*

- *"What would a week of content look like for a cooking Instagram account?"*

✅ Problem Solving:

- *"I'm overwhelmed with my to-do list—can you help me prioritize?"*

- *"Suggest a simple way to organize my digital files and emails."*

- *"How do I handle creative burnout?"*

🛠 Best AI Tools for Coaching and Brainstorming

Tool Name	Role It Plays Clearly	Best Use Cases
ChatGPT	General-purpose coach and idea generator	Personal development, creativity, reflection
Notion AI	Organizational thinking & planning	Projects, tasks, structured goal-setting
MindSmith	Structured decision-making & learning	Personal development, teaching yourself
Reflect AI	Daily journaling and emotional check-ins	Clarity, mindfulness, emotional growth

Clear practical scenario:

You're launching a product but unsure where to start. ChatGPT helps you break the idea into steps, Notion AI organizes the to-do list, and Reflect AI prompts you with daily check-ins to keep momentum going.

🔍 How AI "Coaching" Really Works

AI doesn't give *personalized* advice like a therapist or certified coach, but it can:

- **Guide your thinking** with questions and frameworks

- **Mirror your thoughts back** to help you gain clarity

- **Offer suggestions** you may not have considered

- **Provide encouragement** or motivational reframing

- **Break big ideas into smaller, achievable tasks**

And because it's always available, you can check in whenever inspiration strikes—or doubt creeps in.

💡 Using AI for Creative Brainstorms

Need ideas fast? Here's how AI helps you clearly:

Creative Area	AI Can Help You With...
Writing	Plot twists, character arcs, catchy titles
Business	Slogans, product names, niche ideas
Content	Post themes, carousel breakdowns, campaign ideas
Lifestyle & Wellness	Habit tracking ideas, self-care rituals, routines

Tip: The more specific you are, the more creative AI becomes. Try:

"Brainstorm 5 names for a minimalist skincare line targeting eco-conscious millennials."

"Help me create a 5-day creative reset plan for someone recovering from burnout."

📋 Quick Summary Table: AI as Your Thought Partner

Need	What AI Offers Clearly	Ideal Tool
Goal setting and motivation	Steps, encouragement, reminders	ChatGPT, Reflect AI
Creative brainstorming	Unique ideas, prompts, titles	ChatGPT, Notion AI
Decision support	Pros and cons, frameworks, clarity	MindSmith, ChatGPT
Life or work planning	Priorities, schedules, task breakdowns	Notion AI, Reclaim.ai

▶ Common Misunderstandings Clearly Explained

- ❌ **Myth:** AI replaces personal coaches or therapists
  ✅ **Reality:** AI offers structured thinking support—not emotional counseling or professional advice

- ❌ **Myth:** AI ideas are generic
  ✅ **Reality:** The more detail you give, the more personalized and helpful AI becomes

- ❌ **Myth:** You need a complex prompt to get smart results
  ✅ **Reality:** Even simple requests like *"Help me plan my week"* can unlock surprising clarity

188

Prompt Crafting 101: How to Talk to AI for Better Results

Using AI is like having a powerful assistant—but to get the best out of it, you need to know how to talk to it. The clearer and more intentional your prompt, the better your result.

In this final chapter of the creative expression section, we'll clearly explore how to craft smart, effective prompts that help you get exactly what you want—whether you're writing, designing, planning, researching, or brainstorming.

Good prompts aren't complicated—they're thoughtful, specific, and structured. And with a few simple techniques, you'll know how to guide AI like a pro.

What Is a Prompt, and Why Does It Matter?

A **prompt** is simply your input—the text or question you give to an AI tool. It tells the AI what to generate, how to structure it, what tone to use, and what kind of output you expect.

A good prompt = good results.
A vague prompt = vague answers.

Think of it like ordering at a restaurant:

- Saying *"Bring me food"* might work… but saying *"I'd like a grilled veggie sandwich with no cheese, and a lemon iced tea"* gets you exactly what you want.

 Basic Prompt Formula

You don't need to follow a script—but here's a simple structure you can adapt to almost anything:

[Action] + [Topic or Task] + [Style/Format] + [Tone or Goal]

Examples:

- *Write a motivational quote about creativity in a friendly tone for Instagram.*

- *Create a 3-day meal plan for someone with gluten intolerance, using affordable ingredients.*

- *Summarize this article into 5 bullet points using clear and simple language.*

- *Generate 10 blog post ideas for a wellness coach targeting busy professionals.*

You can mix and match pieces depending on the situation.

✍ Types of Prompts and How to Use Them

Prompt Type	What It's For	Example
Creative Writing	Poems, stories, lyrics	*"Write a four-line poem about hope in the style of haiku"*
Idea Generation	Business, content, names	*"Suggest 10 YouTube channel names for a DIY brand"*
Planning & Lists	Schedules, routines, steps	*"Give me a morning routine to improve focus"*
Explainers	Simplifying complex topics	*"Explain blockchain like I'm 12 years old"*
Role-based	Making AI act in a persona	*"Act as a career coach and help me write a new resume"*

Tip: You can **combine types** for even better results. Example:

"Act as a productivity coach. Help me break down the goal of launching a podcast into weekly tasks. Make the tone encouraging and clear."

🖋 Advanced Prompt Tips for More Precision

1 **Give context.**
   AI performs better when it knows who you are or what the goal is.
   → *"I'm a beginner in fitness. Suggest a simple 5-day workout plan with no equipment."*

2 **Set limits.**
   Ask for a word count, bullet list, time range, or specific format.
   → *"Summarize this in 3 points, each under 15 words."*

3 **Define the audience.**
   AI adjusts tone and complexity based on who it's for.
   → *"Write a LinkedIn post about leadership for startup founders."*

4 **Use examples.**
   If possible, show what you like.
   → *"Here's a tweet I liked—write 3 more in the same style."*

5 **Iterate.**
   Not perfect on the first try? Just ask AI to revise:
   → *"Make it shorter."*
   → *"Add a metaphor."*
   → *"Use a more casual tone."*

🎯 Prompt Crafting by Goal (Quick Guide)

Goal	Example Prompt
Write a post	*"Write a cheerful Instagram caption for a travel photo in Italy."*
Make a list	*"List 7 healthy snacks under 150 calories."*
Learn something	*"Explain how compound interest works in simple terms."*
Create content ideas	*"Give me 10 blog ideas for a parenting coach."*
Get feedback	*"Review my email and suggest a more polite version."*
Visual creation	*"Describe a logo for a modern vegan bakery with warm tones."*

▶ Common Prompting Mistakes (And Fixes)

Mistake	Why It's a Problem	What to Do Instead
Vague prompt	AI guesses—results may be off	Add details, goal, and audience
Too much at once	AI gets confused or generic	Break into smaller tasks or prompts
No follow-up	First answer isn't perfect? Revise!	Give feedback and ask for tweaks

👩 Prompt Crafting as a Skill (That Grows Over Time)

The more you practice, the more intuitive it gets. Prompting is a modern literacy—it teaches you to think clearly, express precisely, and work creatively with technology.

And you don't need to be technical or artistic to master it. Just curious.

SECTION 5

RISKS, ETHICS & THE FUTURE OF AI

(Using AI responsibly and staying informed)

● What Could Go Wrong? Privacy, Deepfakes, and Bias

As powerful and helpful as Artificial Intelligence (AI) can be, it's important to ask a serious question: *What could go wrong?* Like any tool, AI isn't perfect—and when misused or poorly designed, it can cause real harm.

In this chapter, we'll clearly explore the biggest risks associated with AI today. From data privacy issues to deepfake videos to hidden bias, we'll break these topics down simply so you understand not just how to use AI, but how to use it responsibly and stay aware of the challenges it brings.

1. Privacy: What Happens to Your Data?

AI tools often require access to large amounts of information to work well—emails, voice data, search history, user preferences, etc. While this can make AI feel helpful and personalized, it also raises serious concerns about **data privacy**.

Key risks:

- Your conversations with AI tools (like chatbots) may be stored and reviewed for training purposes

- Voice assistants may accidentally "listen in" when they're not supposed to

- Personal data collected by apps might be shared or sold without your knowledge

- Weak data security can lead to leaks or breaches

Simple example:
You use an AI planner that syncs with your calendar, contacts, and notes. If the platform isn't secure—or if it sells data to third parties—your private schedule might not stay so private.

What to do:

- Read privacy policies before sharing sensitive data

- Use tools that allow you to **opt out of data sharing**

- Avoid putting private or sensitive information into AI tools unless you trust the source

- Use platforms that offer **end-to-end encryption**

2. Deepfakes: When AI Makes Fake Look Real

Deepfakes are videos, audio clips, or images created by AI that make people appear to say or do things they never actually did. Some are funny or artistic. Others are used to deceive, manipulate, or cause real harm.

Why they're dangerous:

- Fake videos of politicians or public figures can spread misinformation

- Scammers can impersonate people's voices or faces to commit fraud

- Fake resumes, fake credentials, and fake news can be generated easily

Real-world example:
A finance company received a call from what sounded

like a CEO authorizing a large transfer. It turned out to be a **deepfake voice clone**—and the money was gone.

What to do:

- Verify unexpected audio or video messages, even from known sources

- Use **video authentication tools** or ask for a second confirmation

- Stay skeptical of viral media clips that seem too shocking to be true

⚖️ **3. Bias in AI: The Problem Hiding in the Code**

AI tools learn from data. If the data includes human bias, the AI can unintentionally **repeat or amplify that bias**. That means certain groups may be unfairly treated, excluded, or misrepresented by AI systems.

Examples of AI bias:

- A hiring tool that favors male applicants because it was trained on male-dominated resumes

- A facial recognition system that performs poorly on people with darker skin tones

- A predictive policing system that targets neighborhoods based on flawed historical data

These biases aren't always easy to spot—but they can affect real lives in areas like healthcare, employment, education, and justice.

What to do:

- Support platforms that audit their AI for fairness

- Push for transparency—how was the AI trained? What data was used?

- Be cautious of "black box" tools (those that give results without explanations)

- Stay informed and aware of how decisions are being made—especially if they affect people

Summary Table: AI Risks Clearly Explained

Risk Area	What Could Go Wrong	What You Can Do
Privacy	Data leaks, surveillance, misuse of info	Use secure tools, avoid sharing sensitive data
Deepfakes	Misinformation, scams, identity theft	Verify sources, stay skeptical, use fact-checks
Bias	Unfair decisions in hiring, policing, services	Choose ethical tools, ask for transparency

▶ Other Risk Areas to Watch

- **Automation misuse:** AI used in surveillance, weapons, or mass control

- **Misinformation at scale:** AI can write fake news articles convincingly

- **Mental health effects:** Over-reliance on AI may reduce critical thinking or human interaction

- **Job displacement:** More on this in an upcoming chapter

How to Use AI Safely and Ethically

Artificial Intelligence is changing how we work, learn, create, and communicate. But just like any powerful tool, AI must be used with care. Using it *ethically* means thinking not just about what AI *can* do—but what it *should* do.

In this chapter, we'll clearly explore how to use AI tools in ways that are **safe, fair, and responsible**. Whether you're writing with ChatGPT, designing with DALL·E, or planning your week with an AI assistant, these principles will help you stay in control—and use AI in a way that aligns with your values.

1. Protect Your Privacy

Always remember: **AI tools often store and learn from what you give them.**

Tips for protecting your information:

- **Avoid sharing personal data** like full names, addresses, banking info, medical history, or private messages.

- Use **reputable platforms** that clearly explain how they store and handle your data.

- Choose tools that let you **opt out** of data training and tracking.

- Log out of AI assistants when you're done—or use them in incognito/private mode if available.

🔍 *Example:* Instead of typing, *"Here's my banking info for this invoice,"* ask AI, *"What's the safest way to write an invoice for a freelance project?"*

⚖️ 2. Check for Bias and Fairness

AI can unintentionally reinforce stereotypes, exclude groups, or make unfair suggestions—especially when used in hiring, education, or content moderation.

How to stay fair:

- Don't assume AI is neutral—**review its outputs carefully**.

- Ask: *"Would this result be different if the subject had a different gender, race, or background?"*

- Use inclusive, respectful language when prompting.

- If you're building something with AI (like a chatbot), test it with diverse users to catch blind spots.

👀 *Example:* If AI recommends only male candidates for a leadership role, ask why—and adjust your criteria or data source.

🧠 3. Use AI to Assist, Not Replace Critical Thinking

AI is smart—but it doesn't *understand* the world like humans do. It can make things up, get facts wrong, or take shortcuts.

Best practices:

- **Always double-check facts**, numbers, dates, and references.

- Don't let AI answer on your behalf in high-stakes situations (legal, financial, medical).

- Use AI for *drafts, suggestions, and inspiration*—but apply your own judgment before publishing or acting.

🔧 *Example:* Let AI help you write a business plan—but don't send it to investors without reviewing every line carefully.

✍️ 4. Be Transparent When Using AI

If you create content (articles, videos, art, reports) with the help of AI, it's good practice to **let people know**.

Why transparency matters:

- It builds **trust** with your audience or clients.

- It helps prevent confusion or false impressions.

- It promotes ethical norms in AI use across industries.

📣 *Example:* If you use AI to write your newsletter, you can say:
"This article was edited with the help of AI to save time and stay focused."

5. Respect Intellectual Property

AI tools can mimic styles or generate content that looks or sounds like something that already exists. This raises questions around copyright and ownership.

To stay on the safe side:

- Don't use AI to copy specific artists, voices, or brands without permission.

- When possible, **credit your tools** or sources.

- Avoid passing off AI-generated work as purely original if you didn't do the creative work yourself.

Example: Instead of saying, *"I painted this,"* say, *"This was generated with Midjourney based on my prompt."*

6. Think Before You Automate

AI can handle a lot of tasks: replying to messages, writing emails, making decisions. But just because you *can* automate something doesn't mean you *should*.

Ask yourself:

- Does this task need a **human touch** (e.g. customer support, apologies, creative feedback)?

- Will automation **depersonalize** something important?

- Is there a risk of error, misunderstanding, or offense?

Example: Auto-generating emails to leads might save time—but failing to personalize them could cost trust or opportunity.

Quick Checklist: Ethical AI Use

Guideline	Why It Matters
Don't share private info	Protects your safety and identity
Check AI outputs for bias	Ensures fairness and inclusion
Use your own judgment	Avoids spreading false or flawed information
Be honest about AI use	Builds transparency and trust
Avoid copying or impersonation	Respects creative rights and originality
Keep the human element where needed	Maintains empathy and meaningful connection

 Your Responsibility, Your Power

AI doesn't make ethical decisions—you do.
That's why learning how to use it wisely is one of the most important skills of this decade.

You don't need to be perfect. Just stay thoughtful. Ask questions. Pay attention. And remember: **ethical AI use isn't about limitations—it's about integrity**.

Teaching Kids to Use AI Responsibly

Children are growing up in a world where Artificial Intelligence is everywhere—from voice assistants in the kitchen to chatbots that help with homework. Teaching kids how to use AI is no longer optional—it's essential.

But responsible AI use for kids isn't just about understanding what it *can* do. It's about helping them develop the right habits, boundaries, and awareness so they use technology safely, ethically, and creatively.

In this chapter, we'll clearly explore how to introduce AI to kids of all ages, what risks to watch for, and how to build digital responsibility from the start.

Why Kids Need AI Education (Clearly Explained)

Children will live in an AI-powered future. They may not need to code, but they *will* need to understand:

- What AI is and how it works in daily life

- What it can and can't do

- When to trust it—and when not to

- How to protect their privacy and think critically

Teaching kids about AI is about giving them **confidence, safety, and awareness**—not fear.

How to Explain AI to Kids (By Age Group)

Age Range	How to Teach AI Responsibly
5–8 years	Use simple examples: *"Siri is a robot that listens and helps you."* Encourage curiosity and questions. Emphasize: *"Not everything it says is always right."*
9–12 years	Introduce how AI learns patterns (e.g. YouTube recommendations). Talk about why personal info shouldn't be shared. Encourage asking: *"Who made this?"* and *"Why am I seeing it?"*
13–17 years	Teach privacy, bias, and the difference between AI assistance and human judgment. Discuss plagiarism, deepfakes, and fairness in algorithms. Help them think critically and ethically.

Key Safety Rules for Kids Using AI

1   **Never share private information** with AI tools (names, address, phone numbers).

2   **Always double-check facts**—AI can sound smart but still be wrong.

3   **Ask a trusted adult** before using any new AI-based app or chatbot.

4   **Don't use AI to cheat** on schoolwork—use it to *learn*, not just to get answers.

5   **Be kind**—don't use AI to spread harmful content, bully, or create fake profiles.

Example to share with kids:

"Would you tell a stranger where you live or what school you go to? Then don't type that into an AI chat, either."

Fun and Safe Ways to Explore AI Together

Make AI feel like a **tool for creativity and learning**, not just another screen.

Activity	How to Explore AI Responsibly
Play with voice assistants	Ask questions like "What's the weather?" or "Tell me a joke." Then talk about how the answers are chosen.
Use kid-safe AI apps	Try apps like **Scratch with AI**, **Google's Teachable Machine**, or **Quillionz** for educational fun.
Create art or music with AI	Use tools like **Koodle AI** or **Boomy** to experiment with prompts and ideas.
Compare AI vs real search	Ask the same question to an AI and a search engine. Talk about the differences.
Role-play ethical decisions	Ask: *"Should AI decide who gets a loan?"* or *"Should we believe everything it tells us?"*

Tips for Parents and Educators

- **Set clear boundaries**: When, how, and for what AI can be used

- **Talk openly**: Encourage questions like "Why did the AI say that?"

- **Use parental controls**: Many tools offer AI filters or supervised access

- **Model good behavior**: Show how *you* use AI ethically and responsibly

- **Stay involved**: Ask what AI tools kids are using at school or home

🤖 What NOT to Do

- ❌ Don't treat AI as a babysitter

- ❌ Don't assume the content it generates is always appropriate or accurate

- ❌ Don't allow kids to use AI to copy, cheat, or impersonate

- ❌ Don't introduce AI without teaching digital responsibility

✅ Quick Summary: Teaching Kids AI Responsibility

Principle	What to Teach Kids Clearly
Privacy	Never share names, locations, or passwords
Critical Thinking	Not everything AI says is true or fair
Creativity	Use AI to explore, create, and ask questions
Ethics	Don't use AI to cheat, harm, or mislead others
Parental Support	Always talk about what they're seeing and doing

● Is AI Taking Our Jobs? A Realistic View

It's one of the most common fears people have about Artificial Intelligence:
"Will AI take my job?"
The short answer? **Yes, some jobs will change. Some may even disappear.**
But the full story is more balanced—and more hopeful—than most headlines suggest.

In this chapter, we'll clearly explore what's *really* happening with AI and employment. We'll look at which roles are most affected, which skills are becoming more valuable, and how to prepare for a future where AI is a **partner**, not just a threat.

🏗 What AI Is Already Automating (Clearly Explained)

AI works best on **repetitive, data-driven, predictable** tasks. That means jobs based on rules, patterns, or sorting large amounts of information are most likely to change first.

Examples of roles AI is already affecting:

Role Type	AI Impact
Data entry / admin	AI can auto-fill forms, scan documents, schedule meetings
Customer service	Chatbots handle FAQs and simple issues 24/7
Retail checkout	Self-checkout and smart inventory tools reduce manual roles
Basic content writing	AI writes short product descriptions, captions, summaries
Transportation	Self-driving technology in early testing for trucks, taxis

But here's the key: **AI is replacing tasks, not necessarily entire jobs.**

👷 Which Jobs Are Harder for AI to Replace?

Jobs that involve **creativity, emotional intelligence, problem-solving, or human interaction** are far more resistant to automation.

Examples of more "AI-proof" roles:

- **Healthcare workers** (nurses, therapists, caregivers)

- **Creative professionals** (designers, writers, marketers—with adaptive skills)

- **Trades and technical work** (electricians, mechanics, carpenters)

- **Teachers, trainers, and mentors**

- **Leadership and strategic decision-making roles**

- **Jobs requiring hands-on precision or empathy**

AI can assist these roles—but replacing them completely? Unlikely anytime soon.

How Jobs Are Changing (Not Disappearing)

In many industries, AI isn't eliminating roles—it's **transforming them.**

Example:

- A **marketing manager** now uses AI to analyze trends and write draft campaigns faster.

- A **teacher** uses AI to personalize learning or automate grading—freeing up time for students.

- A **journalist** might use AI to pull research or generate outlines but still writes and edits the final story.

These are not job losses—they're upgrades.

The Jobs AI Is Creating (Yes, Really)

Just like the internet killed some jobs (like travel agents) but created new ones (like app developers), AI is **creating entirely new career paths**, too.

Examples of emerging AI-powered roles:

- **AI trainers** – Teaching AI what "good" responses look like

- **Prompt engineers** – Writing clear, effective prompts to guide AI tools

- **Ethics and policy experts** – Ensuring AI is fair, legal, and safe

- **Data annotators** – Labeling data to train AI

- **AI-assisted creatives** – People who combine AI with design, writing, or music

These jobs require **human intelligence**—paired with AI support.

🎯 Future-Ready Skills to Focus On

To stay ahead in the AI era, focus on what AI *can't* easily replicate:

Skill Type	Why It Matters in the Age of AI
Critical thinking	Evaluating, questioning, refining AI results
Emotional intelligence	Communicating, empathizing, adapting with people
Creativity	Designing, storytelling, innovating
Problem-solving	Tackling unexpected, real-world challenges
Digital fluency	Comfort with AI tools, tech platforms
Collaboration	Teamwork, leadership, cross-functional roles

Quick Summary: AI and Work (Realistic View)

Statement	Truth or Myth?
"AI is replacing all jobs"	✖ Myth. It's replacing **tasks**, not everyone.
"Only tech workers are safe"	✖ Myth. Human-centered skills are just as vital.
"AI is creating new roles"	✅ True. Prompting, ethics, and hybrid roles are growing.
"The future is humans + AI"	✅ True. People who *use* AI will have the advantage.

🚀 How to Future-Proof Yourself

1 **Start learning AI tools now.**
Get comfortable with platforms like ChatGPT, Canva AI, or Notion AI.

2 **Level up your human skills.**
Soft skills matter more than ever in an AI world.

3 **Be flexible.**
The job you'll have in five years might not exist yet —but your ability to adapt is the best insurance.

4 **Think of AI as your intern—not your replacement.**
Let it handle the repetitive parts while you focus on strategy, relationships, and innovation.

● Who Controls AI? Governments, Companies, and You

Artificial Intelligence isn't just shaping our tools—it's shaping our world. But who decides how AI is built, used, and governed? Who sets the limits? Who ensures it's fair, safe, and aligned with human values?

In this chapter, we'll clearly explore **who controls AI today**, what roles governments, tech companies, and regular people like you play in shaping its future—and why your voice matters more than you might think.

🏛 1. Governments: Regulating the Rules (or Trying To)

Governments around the world are just starting to build laws and guidelines for AI, and most are still playing catch-up.

What governments can do:

- **Create AI laws** (e.g. data privacy, discrimination protection, liability)

- **Set safety standards** for tools used in healthcare, finance, transportation, and defense

- **Investigate misuse** of AI (e.g. scams, surveillance, election interference)

- **Support ethical research** and protect public interest

- **Require transparency** about how AI decisions are made

Examples of government actions:

- **European Union:** Leading with the *AI Act*, which classifies AI systems by risk and regulates accordingly

- **U.S. Government:** Creating executive orders, task forces, and ethical AI guidance—but still no national AI law

- **China:** Aggressively developing AI and creating its own regulations focused on state control and data use

📌 *Challenge:* Regulation is slow. Technology moves fast. There's often a big gap between what AI can do and what the law understands.

🧠 2. Big Tech Companies: Building the Tools

Right now, most of the world's AI power is concentrated in the hands of a few large companies. They build the models, run the platforms, and set the terms of use.

Major AI players include:

- **OpenAI** (ChatGPT)

- **Google DeepMind** (Gemini)

- **Meta** (LLaMA)

- **Microsoft** (Azure + OpenAI partnership)

- **Anthropic** (Claude AI)

- **Amazon** (AWS AI, Alexa)

- **Baidu, Alibaba, Tencent** (China-based platforms)

These companies decide:

- What data to train their models on

- How "open" their tools are to the public

- Whether their models are safe, fair, and secure

- What kind of content is allowed or blocked

- How user data is stored and used

⚠️ *Concern:* Corporate incentives don't always align with public interest. Profit, speed, and market dominance often come first.

🙋 3. You: The Everyday User with Real Power

You might not run a tech company—but you still influence how AI grows. How you *use* AI, *talk about* AI, and *vote on* AI-related policies all matter.

Ways you control AI development:

- **Use your voice**: Share feedback, report misuse, demand better standards

- **Choose ethical platforms**: Support companies that value privacy and transparency

- **Teach and model responsibility**: At work, at home, online

- **Advocate for smart policies**: Contact local representatives, support open AI discussions

- **Ask questions**: Who made this tool? How was it trained? What are the risks?

🌍 *Your habits shape the future.* When people demand safe, fair AI, companies and governments respond—because public trust drives adoption.

🧭 What's the Ideal Balance of Power?

AI is too powerful to be left in the hands of *only* governments or *only* corporations. A healthy future depends on **shared responsibility**.

Stakeholder	Role in Shaping AI Clearly
Governments	Protect public interest, set laws, enforce rights
Companies	Innovate responsibly, ensure safety & transparency
People (You)	Use tools wisely, ask questions, demand fairness

🧩 *AI governance is like a puzzle. It only works when every piece is involved.*

📋 Quick Summary: Who Controls AI?

Group	What They Do	Why It Matters
Governments	Regulate safety, fairness, and legal use	Protect citizens and shape public policy
Big Tech Companies	Build the tools, set platform rules	Drive innovation—but need accountability
You	Use, influence, question, educate	Everyday choices shape long-term norms

⬤ AI and Creativity: What's "Real" Anymore?

Can a machine be creative? Can AI make art, music, or stories that move us—like humans do? And if it can... what does that mean for artists, writers, and creators?

In this chapter, we'll clearly explore the **blurry line between human and AI creativity**, how it's shifting our understanding of what's "real," and why creativity in the age of AI is not disappearing—it's evolving.

🎨 What Is Creativity, Really?

Traditionally, creativity means **making something new, meaningful, and original**. It's connected to emotion, inspiration, experience, and intention.

AI, on the other hand, doesn't feel, dream, or imagine. It creates by learning patterns from millions of examples—and remixing them in novel ways.

So is AI *really* creative?

✅ Yes—in a technical sense: It produces new outputs.

❌ But not in a human sense: It doesn't create with purpose, feeling, or personal story.

🤖 How AI "Creates" (Clearly Explained)

AI creativity is powered by **pattern recognition** and **prompt-based generation**.

216

Here's how it works:

1   You give it a **prompt** (e.g. "Draw a sunset over a forest in watercolor style")

2   It searches its training data for similar patterns

3   It generates a **new image, song, poem, or paragraph** by combining those patterns

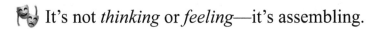 It's not *thinking* or *feeling*—it's assembling.

🎬 Creative Fields Where AI Is Already Active

Field	What AI Can Do Clearly	Example Tools
Visual art	Generate illustrations, logos, style variations	Midjourney, DALL·E, Canva AI
Music	Compose melodies, beats, backing tracks	Boomy, AIVA, Soundraw
Writing	Draft blogs, poems, stories, product copy	ChatGPT, Jasper, Sudowrite
Video	Create short clips, edit footage, animate scenes	Pictory, Runway ML, Synthesia
Design	Generate brand kits, social graphics, UIs	Looka, Adobe Firefly, Tailor Brands

AI helps creators move faster, experiment more, and expand their range—but it also raises big questions.

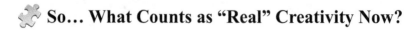 So... What Counts as "Real" Creativity Now?

There's no one-size-fits-all answer. Instead, ask:

- **Who had the idea?** If a human provided the concept and guided the process, that's real creativity—with AI as a tool.

- **Is the story personal or emotional?** AI can generate *style*, but not *story from lived experience*.

- **Does the creator disclose the process?** Transparency matters in building trust with audiences.

A human painting with a brush and a human typing prompts into an AI both count as creative—the intent matters.

⚖ Challenges of AI Creativity

1. **Plagiarism concerns**
   AI might unknowingly copy from real artists or styles without credit.

   Be cautious when using AI for commercial projects—especially with copyrighted material.

2. **Loss of human touch**
   AI-made content can feel flat, generic, or emotionless if not guided well.

3. **Devaluation of original art**
   Some worry that quick, cheap AI content will flood the internet, drowning out human voices.

4   Ethical gray zones
Should someone claim full credit for AI-generated work? Should AI art win awards?

How Creators Are Responding

Response Type	What It Looks Like
Co-creation	Using AI to brainstorm, speed up drafts, enhance ideas
Reinvention	Artists evolving to include AI in their process
Resistance	Some creators reject AI tools completely
Hybrid models	Human writes the lyrics, AI composes the melody (or vice versa)

Ultimately, AI is just another medium—like photography once was. Some feared it would kill painting. It didn't. It *expanded* what art could be.

Quick Summary: AI and Creativity

Question	Simple Answer
Is AI creative?	In a technical way—yes. Emotionally—no.
Can AI replace artists or writers?	Not fully—it lacks soul, context, and story
Should we embrace AI in art?	As a tool, yes. As a substitute, no.
What makes creativity "real"?	Human intention, emotion, and uniqueness

🌱 Your Role in Creative AI

You get to choose:

- Will AI be your shortcut—or your collaborator?

- Will you use it to replace your work—or refine your voice?

- Will you copy what's easy—or create what's *you*?

Creativity in the AI age isn't about competition—it's about reinvention.

● Preparing for the AI Future: Skills You'll Actually Need

The future is not about competing *against* Artificial Intelligence—it's about learning to work *with* it. Whether you're a student, professional, parent, or entrepreneur, AI is becoming part of daily life. The key is knowing how to adapt, stay confident, and remain valuable in a changing world.

In this chapter, we'll clearly explore the **real skills** that will matter most in the AI-powered future. These aren't just technical abilities—they're human strengths that AI can't replace.

🚀 Why Skills Matter More Than Jobs

Technology changes job titles, but **skills are forever**. AI might shift how we do things—but if you have adaptable, transferable skills, you'll stay ready for whatever comes next.

✅ *It's not about becoming a tech expert.*

✅ *It's about learning how to think, learn, and create in new ways.*

Top Skills You'll Actually Need in the AI Future

Skill Category	Why It Matters in an AI World
Critical Thinking	AI gives answers. You need to ask the right questions.
Creativity	AI can remix ideas—but you bring originality, emotion, and vision.
Emotional Intelligence	Human connection, empathy, and communication are irreplaceable.
Digital Fluency	Comfort with using, prompting, and managing AI tools.
Problem Solving	Especially in real-world, unpredictable, or ethical situations.
Collaboration	Working across cultures, disciplines, and with both humans and machines.
Adaptability	The #1 survival skill in any tech-driven world.

 ## AI-Specific Abilities That Are Gaining Value

You don't need to be a coder—but you *should* get comfortable with these:

- **Prompt writing** – Knowing how to guide AI clearly and creatively

- **Tool integration** – Using AI in platforms like Notion, Canva, or Google Docs

- **AI evaluation** – Knowing when an AI output is useful… and when it's not

- **Ethical awareness** – Understanding what's fair, safe, or biased

- **Automation know-how** – Setting up workflows or automating simple tasks

Tip: Start small. Learn one AI tool and build from there.

📚 Learning Path: How to Future-Proof Yourself Step by Step

1 **Pick a task you already do** (writing emails, organizing files, creating content).

2 **Learn how AI can help with it** (e.g., use ChatGPT to outline, Pictory to create videos).

3 **Practice prompting** – Be specific. Experiment with tone, format, and clarity.

4 **Stay curious** – Subscribe to one trusted AI news source or YouTube channel.

5 **Join conversations** – AI is shaping culture. Be part of the discussion.

6 **Teach others** – Explaining AI helps you understand it more deeply.

🎯 Real-World Examples: Skill Meets AI

Role/Field	How Skills and AI Work Together Clearly
Teacher	Uses AI to personalize lessons and save grading time —but keeps human mentorship at the core
Freelancer	Uses AI to draft content, then adds unique brand voice and emotional depth
Healthcare worker	Uses AI for data entry and analysis—but handles all patient interaction with care and empathy
Business owner	Automates emails and inventory—while focusing on customer experience and leadership
Artist or writer	Uses AI for inspiration, not imitation—adds soul to every piece

✅ Mindsets That Make You Future-Ready

- **Lifelong learner** – Stay open to change, not scared of it

- **Tool user, not tool follower** – You control the AI, not the other way around

- **Builder mindset** – Ask: *What can I create with this tool?*

- **Connector** – Combine human and machine strengths for maximum impact

📋 Quick Summary: Future-Ready Skills You'll Actually Use

What to Focus On	Why It Matters
Human strengths	Creativity, empathy, ethics, judgment
AI familiarity	Prompts, tools, basic integration
Critical awareness	Know when to trust, question, or edit AI output
Adaptable mindset	Tech will change—your ability to evolve is key

● Your Next Step: 10 Tools to Try Today + Daily AI Habits

You've made it to the final chapter—well done. Now it's time to move from *learning* to *doing*. AI isn't something you master in one sitting. It's something you get better at, one tool, one prompt, and one habit at a time.

In this closing chapter, you'll find **10 practical AI tools** to start using today, and a set of **simple daily habits** to help you stay confident, creative, and in control as the world continues to evolve around Artificial Intelligence.

Let's clearly begin.

10 AI Tools to Try Today (Beginner-Friendly)

These tools are easy to start with, don't require coding, and offer immediate value for your daily life, work, or creativity.

Tool Name	What It Helps You Do Clearly	Website
ChatGPT	Write, brainstorm, ask questions, plan	chat.openai.com
Canva AI	Design graphics, presentations, social posts	canva.com
Pictory	Turn text or blogs into short videos	pictory.ai
Looka	Design logos and brand kits	looka.com
Copy.ai	Write captions, emails, product descriptions	copy.ai
Runway ML	Edit videos with AI, remove backgrounds	runwayml.com
Notion AI	Organize projects, take smart notes	notion.so
Boomy	Create original music tracks with AI	boomy.com
Grammarly AI	Check grammar, tone, clarity, and rewrite	grammarly.com
Soundraw	Generate music for videos or podcasts	soundraw.io

✅ *Start with just 1–2 tools. Use them to solve a real problem or enhance a real project you're working on.*

📅17 5 Daily AI Habits for Beginners

These small, simple habits will help you get comfortable with AI without overwhelm.

1. Ask One Smart Question a Day

Use ChatGPT or another chatbot to explore something new:

- *"Summarize this news article in 5 bullet points."*

- *"Explain quantum physics like I'm 12."*

2. Practice One Prompt a Day

Try asking an AI to do something creative, fun, or practical:

- *"Plan a 3-day healthy meal plan on a budget."*

- *"Write a joke about coffee in the style of a pirate."*

3. Review Before You Trust

Any time you get an AI result, double-check the facts or logic. This builds critical thinking as a habit.

4. Try a New Tool Weekly

Pick one new AI app or platform each week and experiment for 10 minutes. You'll build confidence fast.

5. Reflect on What Feels Useful

At the end of the week, ask yourself:

- *What AI tool helped me most?*

- *What do I want to try next?*

⊘ What Comes Next?

You don't need to become an AI expert. You just need to:

- **Stay curious**

- **Practice intentionally**

- **Adapt openly**

- **Think ethically**

AI is not here to replace you. It's here to work *with* you—if you're ready.

"The future isn't about man vs. machine. It's about man with machine, creating more than either could alone."

You now have the knowledge, tools, and mindset to thrive in a world shaped by AI. Stay thoughtful. Stay creative. And take the next step—starting today.

Thank you for reading *The Power of AI* — a simple, practical, and no-hype guide to understanding and using Artificial Intelligence to improve everyday life. This book was designed to make AI accessible, useful, and empowering for anyone—no technical background required.

In a world where technology is changing rapidly, clarity and confidence are more important than ever. The goal of this guide has been to equip readers with the tools and mindset needed to engage with AI thoughtfully—whether for work, learning, creativity, or daily routines.

If this book has been helpful, insightful, or inspiring, a brief review on Amazon would be sincerely appreciated. Even a few words can help others discover the book and benefit from it, just as you have.

Thank you again for reading — and here's to making the most of the future, one smart decision at a time.

— **MASTERPLANNERS Team**

www.ingramcontent.com/pod-product-compliance
Lightning Source LLC
LaVergne TN
LVHW051227050326
832903LV00028B/2278